AFFIRMATIVE ACTION
IN THE EMPLOYMENT
OF ETHNIC MINORITIES
AND PERSONS WITH DISABILITIES

AFFIRMATIVE ACTION IN THE EMPLOYMENT OF ETHNIC MINORITIES AND PERSONS WITH DISABILITIES

Edited by Jane Hodges-Aeberhard and Carl Raskin

International Labour Office   Geneva

BKL 9577-7/1

Aeberhard-Hodges, J.; Raskin, C.
Affirmative action in the employment of ethnic minorities and persons with disabilities
Geneva, International Labour Office, 1997

/Case study/, /affirmative action/, /employment opportunity/, /equal opportunity/, /ethnic group/, /minority group/, /disabled person/, /Canada/, /India/, /Lebanon/, /Malaysia/, /Norway/, /Philippines/, /Russian Federation/, /Uganda/. 04.02.2
ISBN 92-2-109521-5

ILO Cataloguing in Publication Data

Printed in Switzerland

ART

FOREWORD

To many, in particular to disability rights advocates, it may seem awkward to analyse the employment situation of persons with disabilities together with that of ethnic minorities. Is it legitimate to subsume individuals who belong to either of these two groups, together with many other individuals and social groups, under the term disadvantaged or vulnerable? Is vulnerability an attribute? Is it justified to view the problems that people with disabilities experience as being comparable to the disadvantage that people belonging to ethnic minorities have?

This book is not concerned with describing categories of people or with analysing social policies for specific population groups. The case-studies it contains approach the issue of disadvantage from a discrimination perspective. And this reveals a shocking truth: disadvantage is to a great measure the avoidable product of other peoples' behaviour and action; vulnerability is first and foremost the result of denied opportunities and unjustifiable social exclusion. Beyond all differences, this propensity to be treated differently is what makes individuals become part of a vulnerable group and experience social and occupational disadvantages.

Answers to these problems, then, cannot be charity or welfare, but first and foremost changes in peoples' behaviour. Such changes do not occur easily and need to be backed up by affirmative action that counteracts the effects of discrimination. What countries do, or do not do, to deal with the various forms of discrimination is witnessed in the various country reports that make up this book.

However, the commonality of facing obstacles in gaining access to employment opportunities should not conceal that there are substantive differences in the way in which the actors who control the labour market, as well as governments, perceive and treat such groups. It is the merit of this book to look beyond generalities and not to be satisfied with offering yet another piece of evidence of discriminatory practices in general, but to present us with a detailed picture of the situation in selected countries and, in particular, of the affirmative action measures that have been put in place to redress injustices.

Here we discover that people with disabilities may see their struggle for equal treatment in employment frustrated because of lack of knowledge about their abilities or even because of sympathy for their "suffering", whereas people belonging to ethnic minorities are more likely to face outright hostility and less decisive government support in their favour. I am certain that such differences could trigger some useful reflections among those of us who see disabled people as the major or exclusive target of discrimination and display little concern for other groups struggling for fair treatment. This book should remind us that the solution cannot be to seek preferential situations for specific groups, but to denounce and combat discriminatory policies and practices on all fronts, irrespective of which group has managed to gain official protection against discrimination.

We owe this book to a collaborative effort by the Equality and Human Rights Coordination Branch and the Vocational Rehabilitation Branch of the ILO; to the editors Jane Hodges-Aeberhard (Equality and Human Rights Coordination Branch) and Carl Raskin (then of Human Resources Development, Canada, on secondment to the ILO Ottawa Office) but more importantly to the readiness and ability of the eight authors — some of whom have asked to keep their anonymity — to research and give accounts of discrimination and affirmative action practices regarding these two so different groups in their countries.

Willi Momm,
Chief, Vocational Rehabilitation Branch,
International Labour Office

CONTENTS

Chapter 8

Chapter 9

INTRODUCTION

This publication of the International Labour Office's Equality and Human Rights Coordination Branch assesses the affirmative action programmes in place in several countries throughout the world that seek to overcome discrimination in employment experienced by ethnic minorities and persons with disabilities. It follows on from Professor Faundez's 1994 publication, *Affirmative action: International perspectives,*[1] which examined the concept of affirmative action — or positive action (as it is sometimes called) — from both a philosophical and a theoretical economic perspective.

Many countries have special measures in place that mandate the taking of affirmative action on behalf of persons with disabilities and ethnic minorities. The programmes flow from the observation that merely prohibiting discrimination is often insufficient to eliminate the *de facto* practice. Positive measures, then, may be seen as steps which "set out to eliminate and make good any *de facto* inequalities, thereby enabling members of groups suffering from discrimination or disadvantage to work in all sectors of activity and at all levels of responsibility".[2] They are usually targeted at specific groups and in place for a limited period of time.

However, affirmative action programmes vary greatly, in terms of both their underlying rationale, and the manner in which they are put into operation, or delivered. This book aims, via an examination of national case-studies, to discuss the different ways in which these initiatives are carried out and highlight successes or weaknesses.

First, it must be noted that the controversy surrounding the concept of affirmative action, particularly the view that it constitutes reverse discrimination, already noted by Faundez, resurfaces in the case-studies. While the chapter on Canada shows that the quandary of viewing equality as "sameness" has been alleviated by treating persons as equals by accommodating their differences, the Malaysian and Indian experiences point to resentment felt by groups not benefiting from such measures. In the Philippines, a major law for the disabled was adopted with the reservation of certain posts in the public service, despite debate in Congress against this type of "special dispensation".

With reference to the rationale for affirmative action, the scheme found in Canada, for example, is a legislatively based initiative that builds on existing anti-discrimination statutes. The programme seeks, in a comprehensive fashion, to attain labour market levels of representation and participation for disabled persons and ethnic minorities that are equitable compared to those experienced by the population at large. A component of Canada's programme is the requirement that enterprises undertake detailed analyses of their workforces, as well as elaborate plans to identify and eliminate structural barriers that inhibit disabled persons and ethnic minorities from securing employment and advancement in the workplace.

In other States, such as Lebanon, the affirmative action measures were enacted not so much as a response to structural discrimination in the workplace, but rather as a way to address imbalances in the distribution of power along sectarian and religious lines that had contributed to the civil disorders which ravaged the country from 1975 to 1991. In response to the strife, an agreement was reached in 1989 whereby a new formula for the distribution of power along sectarian lines was agreed upon among the various religions and political leaders of the time. Government policies, including employment policies, must be drawn up in accordance with this policy, which will remain in effect until religious sectarianism is no longer a part of the system.

In still other jurisdictions, such as the Russian Federation, affirmative action may be seen as a response to economic dislocations experienced by disadvantaged groups — young people, women and persons with disabilities — as well as ways to quell ethnic tensions from national groups who had previously lacked official recognition.

OPERATIONAL PERSPECTIVES

Much as the rationale for instituting affirmative action in employment may vary, so too do the methods by which these programmes are operationalized. The implementation varies for the two groups targeted by this study.

For persons with disabilities, on the one hand, the disadvantages and discrimination they face are based on fundamentally different causes from those experienced by ethnic minorities. Disabled persons rarely experience barriers to employment as a result of overt hostility. In fact, such discrimination often takes place with the best of intentions, and genuine concern about their capabilities and a desire to protect them from harm, injury or embarrassment. Strong comments are made in the Malaysian case-study on the need to change this attitude of "charity" towards the disabled as it reinforces a belief that they are incapable of becoming part of the open labour market. In response to this reality, affirmative action on behalf of persons with disabilities frequently takes the form of quota systems, which require that a certain percentage of jobs be set aside for persons with disabilities.[3] Such quotas may be applicable to either the public or private sector, or to both.

The systems in place in many of the countries profiled in this publication follow this approach. For example, in Malaysia, 1 per cent of positions in the public and private sector are reserved for persons with disabilities; in the Philippines, 5 per cent of certain positions in departments or offices engaged in social development are reserved for disabled individuals; in Russia, state employment bodies must establish specialized groups for the occupational rehabilitation of, and provision of employment for, disabled individuals; in Lebanon, a proposed quota would enforce the employment of disabled persons in both the public and private sectors through the adoption of a 4 per cent quota. Moreover, the quota system may contain a penalty levy if the enterprise does not hire the requisite number of disabled persons. Such an approach is being considered by Lebanon.

Care, of course, has to be taken when developing employment policy through quota legislation, in the form in which it is usually defined and practised in developing countries. In many such cases, the effect of such legislation is that enterprises understand it to mean that they have a duty to take on a certain percentage of workers with reduced working capacity. Employers will therefore see the law as acting against good economic sense and might be inclined to resent and to circumvent it. Only in combination with a human resource development policy which first develops the skills and competencies of disabled workers before placing them or with support to workplace-based training under a "supported employment programme" can quota systems be regarded as an effective measure of affirmative action.* There is an ongoing controversy about the appropriateness of quota legislation for the disabled and many call for the introduction of anti-discrimination legislation as the better policy solution. However, the blending of affirmative action measures of many kinds, against the backdrop of equality laws, is probably the trend in many countries these days.**

On the other hand, ethnic minorities have often been subjected to overtly prejudicial treatment. As such, the national studies in this publication demonstrate the need for responses that recognize this fundamental fact. For example, in Canada, ethnic minorities are not designated under the affirmative action programme. Rather, the programme specifies persons who are considered to be "visible minorities" — a racial connotation. In India, the Constitution bans discrimination on the ground of caste and makes provision for the reservation of certain posts for the "backward class" of citizens not represented in the service of the State. And, in Malaysia, the Government recognized that the indigenous Malay population experienced economic deprivation. In response, it introduced a quota system in areas such as admission to universities, equity ownership, and employment and promotion in the public service. This programme was meant to be in place for a 20-year period. In the United States, on the other hand, the legislation is not based on a quota system, but rather requires employers "to take affirmative action to employ and advance workers with disabilities". The American programme also requires employers to modify their worksites to "reasonably accommodate" persons with disabilities.

* As is the case in Germany and France.

** Note, however, that some countries with strong equality laws provide for relatively weak or no affirmative action measures for the disabled. This is traditionally so in some Scandinavian countries, but is also the case in Australia, the United States and the United Kingdom which have recently adopted anti-discrimination legislation for this group. For example, the United Kingdom 1995 Disability Discrimination Act repeals the quota system previously in force in that country, to the chagrin of some commentators: see B. Doyle, 1996.

METHODOLOGY

Most of the case-studies attempt a definition or characterization of the two groups targeted in this book. Thus Article 1 of the ILO's Vocational Rehabilitation and Employment (Disabled Persons) Convention, 1983 (No. 159), keeps a labour market flavour in its definition: "For the purposes of this Convention, the term 'disabled person' means an individual whose prospects of securing, retaining and advancing in suitable employment are substantially reduced as a result of a duly recognized physical or mental impairment". Some studies, however, preferred to use the 1980 World Health Organization's International Classification of Impairments, Disabilities and Handicaps.[4] Others referred to the United Nations Standard Rules on the Equalization of Opportunities for Persons with Disabilities[5] or the definition in the World Programme of Action concerning disabled persons.[6] Still others preferred to remain within the scope of domestic legal definitions.

For ethnic minorities, some case-studies refer to ratification of the Discrimination (Employment and Occupation) Convention, 1958 (No. 111), and the Indigenous and Tribal Peoples Convention, 1983 (No. 169). The former relates to, without defining them, colour, race and national extraction. The latter relates to "tribal peoples ... whose social, cultural and economic conditions distinguish them from other sections of the national community, and whose status is regulated wholly or partially by their own customs or traditions or by special laws or regulations", as well as "peoples ... who are regarded as indigenous on account of their descent from the populations which inhabited the country" in question, "or a geographical region to which the country belongs, at the time of conquest or colonization or the establishment of present state boundaries and who, irrespective of their legal status, retain some or all of their own social, economic, cultural and political institutions".

Most case-studies, however, use the national definitions and even common usage. This gives rise to an interesting diversity of approaches to the research: given that the Sami of Norway are recognized as an indigenous people rather than an ethnic minority, that case-study does not include them in its analysis of programmes which exist, in any case, mostly for immigrants of non-Norwegian origin. Yet the Russian case-study uses a similar definitional approach to restrict its analysis to only the numerically small peoples of the North of Russia, who are recognized as indigenous and tribal peoples. The Malaysian chapter also reflects the legal definition of one particular group, which includes indigenous peoples of quite varied origins. According to the Philippine study, the term ethnic minorities is used interchangeably for national minorities and indigenous peoples.

Certain case-studies also take a very broad definition of employment-related issues, in particular in describing affirmative action for ethnic minorities. They include sociological analyses and assess land rights and general infrastructure needs given that the target groups are indigenous peoples surviving in a subsistence economy (Philippines, Uganda). This approach is clearly justified in terms of Convention No. 169 — which encourages action beyond the formal labour market for these peoples' development — and in terms of the holistic nature of certain countries' policies to eliminate discrimination. More is said on the success of this overall approach as a means of contributing to ethnic minorities' chances of gaining employment, whether in the traditional or modern economy, in the conclusions to this volume.

The methodological approaches that have been used by the authors in presenting the various national affirmative action programmes include:

— a review and analysis of the legislative and/or policy statements that constitute the formal programme;

— a review of labour court and tribunal decisions;

— examining collective agreements;

— examining and analysing policies of various corporate entities and trade unions;

— preparing and circulating a questionnaire for use in interviews of heads of various bodies working in the fields covered by the study;

— conducting interviews with academics, representatives of workers' and employers' organizations, persons involved in the application of enterprise affirmative action policies, groups representing persons with disabilities and ethnic minorities and voluntary non-governmental organizations (NGOs), as well as government officials who administer affirmative action legislation;

— visits to employment exchanges established particularly for one of the target groups; and

— reviewing and analysing empirical studies.

Several studies bemoan the lack of statistical data (Canada, India, Malaysia, the Philippines, Norway, the Russian Federation), which can lead to problems in pinpointing groups deserving of affirmative action or which, more importantly in the context of this book, makes it almost impossible to evaluate — in quantitative terms — the impact of programmes which incorporate quotas or targets for such groups.

Notes

[1] Faundez, 1994.

[2] ILO, 1988, p. 177.

[3] For a discussion of quotas see B. Doyle, 1993.

[4] WHO, 1980.

[5] United Nations, 1993b.

[6] idem, 1982.

CANADA
Carl Raskin*

1

Canada's affirmative action programme at the federal level differs from many of the other measures being used throughout the world, in that it groups together four designated groups — women, aboriginal peoples, persons with disabilities and visible minorities — into one comprehensive inclusive measure.[1] The Canadian programme is known as employment equity, but for clarity's sake is referred to here as affirmative action. It is not a quota system; rather, the Canadian approach is seen to be a process by which structural barriers that create discriminatory disadvantages in employment are removed.[2] The federal affirmative action programme is but one of many affirmative action measures that are in effect across the country. Various municipalities have affirmative action programmes in place; another measure covers public servants in the Provinces of British Columbia and Saskatchewan; a voluntary programme is in place in Quebec; and legislation establishing a comprehensive affirmative action programme was passed in Canada's largest Province, Ontario, and became law on 1 September 1994. However, while the federal measure is solely applicable to enterprises and organizations that come under federal jurisdiction, it is the only one that is uniformly applicable across the country, and has been subject to an extensive review process.

This chapter examines the affirmative action programmes under the Employment Equity Act and the Federal Contractors Programme. The equality provision of the Charter of Rights and Freedoms does not contain a structured programme component. Similarly, the Canadian Human Rights Act (CHRA) merely authorizes individual enterprises to engage in positive measures on a voluntary basis and is not an organized affirmative action programme as such.

I. LEGISLATIVE OVERVIEW AND HISTORICAL PERSPECTIVE

The concept of affirmative action was first introduced in the 1978 CHRA, which bans individual acts of discrimination in employment as well as the pursuit of discriminatory employment policies and practices based on

* Then of Human Resource Development, Canada, on secondment to the ILO Ottawa Office.

ten grounds including national or ethnic origin, colour and disability (sections 7 and 10). The Act also allows organizations to adopt or carry out what are deemed to be "special programmes" designed to prevent or eliminate disadvantages that may be suffered by any group of individuals when those disadvantages are related to one of the ten grounds of discrimination found in the Act (section 16(1)). The CHRA, then, provides for a kind of "voluntary" affirmative action. Provincial anti-discrimination legislation closely mirrors its federal counterpart. For example, in Ontario, the Human Rights Code also has a provision that authorizes special programmes that are permissive, not mandatory.

In 1982, Canada's Constitution was amended to include a section known as the Charter of Rights and Freedoms, which codified fundamental liberties (Constitution Act, 1982). The equality provision (section 15) offers protection against discrimination by the actions of government and enshrines affirmative action measures. However, the Charter is only applicable to the actions of government and does not establish a stand-alone affirmative action programme. Persons who believe they have been victims of discrimination must complain to a human rights commission.[3]

Despite the anti-discrimination legislation in place, it became clear that the existing statutes could not deal with the structural or "systemic" discrimination in the Canadian workplace experienced by women, visible minorities, disabled persons and aboriginal peoples. Following rec-ommendations contained in the report of the 1984 Royal Commission on Equality in Employment, chaired by Judge Rosalie Abella, and of the Parliament of Canada's Standing Committee on Justice and Legal Affairs, which reviewed the equality section of the Charter of Rights and Freedoms, the Employment Equity Act was passed in 1986.

II. REQUIREMENTS OF THE EMPLOYMENT EQUITY ACT

The legislation mandates the institution of positive policies and practices to ensure that persons in designated groups (women, aboriginal peoples, persons with disabilities and persons who are visible minorities in Canada) "achieve a degree of representation in the various positions of employment with the employer that is at least proportionate to their representation: (i) in the workforce; or (ii) in those segments of the workforce that are identifiable by qualification, eligibility or geography and from which the employer may reasonably be expected to draw or promote employees".[4] In Canada there is thus no quota scheme on behalf of persons who are members of designated groups. Rather, the Canadian programme seeks the attainment of an "equitable" workforce.

The Canadian affirmative action legislation calls upon employers:

— to eliminate practices that result in systemic or structural employment barriers;

— to institute measures that will ensure that persons who belong to one of the four designated groups subject to the employment equity law achieve a degree of representation in the various positions of employment with the employer that is proportionate to their representation in the workforce; and

— to prepare yearly plans that outline the employment equity goals that they propose to achieve as well as timetables for implementing them.

Covered by the legislation are organizations of 100 or more employees under federal jurisdiction, the exceptions being private works in the Yukon and Northwest Territories or a corporation that is a government department.[5] There are in Canada 345 employers under federal jurisdiction subject to the Employment Equity Act that in 1993 encompassed 603,000 jobs.[6] The Government has a separate employment equity programme for its own employees, known as the "Special Measures Programme", that is not discussed in this paper.

A key element of Canada's affirmative action programmes is the notion of "self-identification". In compiling the workforce analysis, it is the employee and not the employer who "self-identifies" whether he/she is a member of a designated group. With reference to the two groups studied in this chapter, the Canadian affirmative action measures define persons with disabilities as having: "(i) ... persistent physical, mental, psychiatric, sensory or learning impairment ...; (ii) consider themselves to be, or believe that an employer or potential employer would be likely to consider them to be, disadvantaged in employment by reason of an impairment referred to in subparagraph (i); and (iii) ... identify themselves to an employer, or agree to be identified by an employer as persons with disabilities ...". On the other hand, Canada's affirmative action measures do not offer protection to "ethnic minorities", but rather to "persons other than aboriginal peoples, who are, because of their race or colour, in a visible minority in Canada are considered to be persons who are non-Caucasian in race or non-white in colour ...".[7] Not all immigrant workers or ethnic minorities are visible minorities. However, a majority of immigrants to Canada (59.7 per cent for available 1990 statistics) come from visible minority source countries in Africa/Middle East and Asia. In essence, for Canada, discrimination on the basis of being a migrant worker implies discrimination on the grounds of race and colour and national or ethnic origin, thus a visible minority.[8] Therefore, the term (ethnic) visible minority is used in the remainder of this chapter.

The federal Employment Equity Act does not contain any enforcement provisions. Rather, pursuant to section 6 of the Act, employers are only required to send an annual report to the responsible minister, failing which they may be fined up to Can$50,000. However, these employer reports are, in fact, public documents and they form the basis of the annual "Employment Equity Report" published by the federal Department of Human Resources Development. This document summarizes the performance of the employers under the jurisdiction of the legislation.

Section 8 of the Employment Equity Act requires that a copy of the report be provided to the Canadian Human Rights Commission (CHRC).

While the CHRC is under no statutory obligation to do anything with the report once it is received, it has established a policy: to investigate any reasonable third party complaint, based upon data produced under the Act; to invite employers whose workforce representation of designated groups is low to participate in a joint review of their employment systems; and to initiate a complaint if the employer rejects a joint review.[9]

Under the Federal Contractors' Programme (FCP), established by the Government for enterprises with which it does business, suppliers of goods and services who may not necessarily be subject to the Employment Equity Act (such as employers who come under the jurisdiction of the various provincial governments) but who employ more than 100 employees and bid on contracts of Can$200,000 or more, must implement employment equity for the four designated groups. Companies must agree to a number of activities that promote employment equity, including collecting and compiling information on the workforce, establishing a system to track hiring, promotion, training and termination, establishing goals for designated group employees and developing an employment equity workplan. The programme provides for monitoring and compliance review procedure by the federal Government. Companies that fail to respect their engagements can be subjected to sanctions, including eventual exclusion from bidding on federal government contracts.[10]

It must be clearly understood that the focus of Canada's affirmative action programmes is on the detailed reporting of employment data by enterprises. Neither the Employment Equity Act nor the FCP require the hiring of anyone!

III. THE LABOUR MARKET PORTRAIT OF (ETHNIC) VISIBLE MINORITIES AND PERSONS WITH DISABILITIES

Canadian practice has established four criteria against which an equitable labour force (by extension for persons with disabilities and (ethnic) visible minorities) may be measured:[11]

— unemployment: that the levels of unemployment for persons with disabilities and (ethnic) visible minorities should be no higher than the respective rate of the general workforce;

— occupational representation: that the presence of disabled persons and (ethnic) visible minorities at all levels of the workforce be equal to their representation in the general population commensurate with their availability in a given occupation;

— income: that income levels for persons with disabilities and (ethnic) visible minorities should be equal to those of the general population;

— participation: that persons with disabilities and (ethnic) visible minorities experience a level of workforce participation comparable to the general population.

The following labour force portrait demonstrates that persons with disabilities and (ethnic) visible minorities have yet to achieve an equitable working environment when compared to the population at large.

Persons with disabilities

The participation and occupational representation of persons with disabilities was, in 1992, 2.54 per cent of the workforce covered by the Employment Equity Act. This is much lower than 5.4 per cent, which is their share of the Canadian workforce as a whole. The Health and Activities Limitation Survey reports that of the 2,297,135 disabled Canadians between the ages of 15 and 64, 56.3 per cent participate in the labour force; this compares to a participation rate of 80.8 per cent for persons without disabilities.[12] While disabled persons were under-represented in nearly every occupation and in every industrial sector, their occupational patterns were consistent with the general workforce under the legislation. Persons with disabilities were overrepresented in clerical positions (20.42 per cent of disabled men were clerical workers compared to 14.91 per cent of all men; 66.17 per cent of women with disabilities were clerical workers compared to 60.45 per cent of all women). They were under-represented in blue-collar trades and technical jobs.[13]

The full-time recruitment of persons with disabilities (1.34 per cent) was slightly greater in 1992 than in 1991 (1.13 per cent), but it remains much lower than their representation in the full-time workforce; terminations over recruitment actually reduced the percentage number of disabled persons in the workforce covered by the Employment Equity Act by 4.81 per cent. Moreover, during the last six years, the recruitment rate of disabled persons has been "consistently lower" than its representation in the workforce under the Act.[14]

The salaries of persons with disabilities closely resembled those of all persons in the workforce covered by the Act. Disabled women earned $31,622, or 95.44 per cent of all womens' pay. Disabled men earned on average $44,235, or 98.24 per cent of all mens' pay.[15] However, it must be recalled that the workforce covered by the federal affirmative action legislation accounts for only about 10 per cent of the total Canadian labour force. Moreover, these figures represent employed disabled persons. When the total disabled population is considered, adults with disabilities are just over half as likely as non-disabled adults to have earnings of $35,000 or better, and are much more likely to have incomes of less than $10,000 than non-disabled persons.[16]

(Ethnic) visible minorities

The participation and occupational representation level of (ethnic) visible minorities in enterprises covered by the federal employment equity legislation was 7.91 per cent in 1992. (Ethnic) visible minorities are well represented as full-time middle managers (14.96 per cent male, and 12.41 per cent female) but are over-represented as professionals (17.2 per cent (ethnic) visible minority male v. 6.69 per cent of all men under the Act worked in this occupational group) and as clerical workers (11.40 per cent).

However, they are greatly under-represented as upper-level managers (0.69 per cent of male (ethnic) visible minorities v. 1.58 per cent of all males under the Act and 0.09 per cent of women (ethnic) visible minorities as compared to 0.24 per cent of all women) and in blue-collar and technical trades.[17] In the general population, the 1991 census concerning the occupational representation of (ethnic) visible minorities also indicates that they are significantly under-represented in upper-level and middle management, as foremen/women, and in skilled and semi-skilled trades.

For Canada as a whole, the unemployment rate reported in the 1991 Census was 10.2 per cent, with an overall workforce participation rate of 67.9 per cent, whereas (ethnic) visible minorities have an unemployment rate of 13.1 per cent, with a 70.5 per cent participation rate.

For (ethnic) visible minority persons employed in enterprises under the Employment Equity Act, the estimated average full-time salary in 1992 for women was $32,075 or 96.68 per cent of the average salary of all women. Male (ethnic) visible minority employees earned $42,296, or 93.93 per cent of the average salary for all men.[18] The unemployment and participation rates must be examined in terms of income and occupational segregation. Raskin citing Samuel[19] notes that this is an indicator of discrimination against migrants. If a higher percentage of a certain group work, yet have economic outcomes that are lower, then there is a discriminatory effect for that group.[20]

IV. THE IMPACT AND EFFECTIVENESS OF THE FEDERAL AFFIRMATIVE ACTION PROGRAMME

During 1992, a Special Parliamentary Committee reviewed the federal affirmative action legislation. Employers noted that they were often unable to find qualified candidates, whereas representatives of designated groups, especially persons with disabilities, felt the failure to put supportive measures in place has provided employers with an excuse for not implementing workplace equity. The Special Committee echoed the concerns of both, noting that "... employment equity should be combined with labour force development strategies, training strategies, labour relations and education ... Lasting solutions to the employment problems of disadvantaged groups will come only from attacking the root causes of employment inequity".[21]

The concerns expressed to the Special Committee, together with the labour force portrait of persons with disabilities and (ethnic) visible minorities, might lead one to conclude that the affirmative action legislation has not been effective in having an impact on individual enterprises and Canadian society. Such an impression would be erroneous. Rather, the impacts of the federal programmes have resulted in a complex set of outcomes. The labour market is not yet equitable and many enterprises outside (and inside) the ambit of the federal legislation have yet to implement affirmative action programmes, or have not fully understood or committed themselves to the affirmative action process. That said, it is argued that the process engendered by the putting into place of mandatory affirmative action programmes has created a climate where equity issues are high on the Canadian agenda, and that such a process must, inexorably, lead to profound changes in the workplace, including corporate and union cultures. Such change is manifested in diverse ways, such as the inclusion of affirmative action clauses in collective agreements, the reaching of "joint agreement" settlements between employers and the CHRC, the elaboration of "good practices", qualitative measures by employers' and workers' organizations and worker training.

Collective agreements

A number of collective agreements contain affirmative action provisions; two such agreements are presented here for comparison.

The agreement between the Windsor Roman Catholic Separate School Board and the Ontario English Catholic Teachers' Association dated 1 September 1992 (1 September 1992 to 31 August 1994) stipulates:

> 1.04 The Board agrees that all teachers shall have equal opportunity for teaching positions of added responsibility consistent with the Board's commitment to Affirmative Action/Employment Equity Programmes.

The 25 October 1990 agreement between Chrysler Canada Ltd. and the Canadian Auto Workers (CAW) contains detailed sections dealing with aspects of affirmative action/employment equity, and starts with the assertion that "... During current negotiations, the parties reaffirmed the policy of the company and the CAW [...] that the provisions of the agreement be applied to all employees covered by the agreement without regard to race, colour, religion, age, sex, national origin or handicap. Additionally, the company reaffirmed its policy to extend opportunities for employment and advancement within the company to all qualified applicants and employees on a non-discriminatory basis." That agreement provides that a local affirmative action committee will be established at each plant location whose activities shall include community school visits so as to widen the recruitment pool and encouragement of further training for current staff with special emphasis on women, visible minorities, native Canadian people and the handicapped.

The agreement recognized that local committees will require ongoing assistance and direction and therefore provided that a master affirmative action committee will be established, consisting of two members of the national union and two staff members of the company. This committee will meet quarterly and may be supplemented, by mutual agreement, by local committee representatives.

One is struck by the difference in detail in the above agreements: one simply voices support for the principles of affirmative action; the other provides a structure and elaborate guidelines. If the contents of collective agreements can be indicative of the steps employers and workers take together to achieve employment equity, then these broad differences in the way they address the issue may be symptomatic of a failure to understand what must be done as part of the affirmative action process. In fact, several observers have remarked that the legislation, while requiring enterprises to prepare employment equity plans, does not clearly distinguish what constitutes successful elements of such a plan. Moreover, the failure of the legislation to indicate in clear terms what is expected may be one reason why performance has been so "uneven".[22] It should be noted, however, that these two affirmative action agreements came into effect before the proclamation of Ontario's mandatory programme. Is not the fact that ·^h firms have agreed to negotiate such provisions into labour contracts a stı ong indication that the affirmative action programmes create climates that increase the level of awareness and lead to change?

Courses and workshops provided by workers' organizations

In order to sensitize their members, Canadian labour unions offer workshops and courses concerning affirmative action. The following are exemplary. The Public Service Alliance of Canada (PSAC), the nation's largest civil service union, has developed several formal weekend and evening courses that sensitize its membership concerning various aspects of the affirmative action process. In addition, at the request of its locals, PSAC will develop specifically designed course modules for presentation. It is able to call upon a network of individuals composed of target group members (such as persons with disabilities and (ethnic) visible minorities) who will provide informal training.[23] The Canadian Labour Congress (CLC), the nation's largest labour federation, currently provides affirmative action components as a part of its courses on human rights (anti-discrimination). The CLC is in the process of developing stand-alone affirmative action courses, especially for its smaller affiliated unions that do not now have the capacity to furnish courses independently. It has also integrated affirmative action into its general courses.[24] The Canadian Union of Public Employees (CUPE), the nation's largest public sector union, provides a number of affirmative action courses through its education department. There is a general employment equity course; a course entitled "Breaking through barriers" which addresses all four designated groups, but for women only; an anti-racism and cross-cultural awareness course; and a course concerning persons with disabilities. Also, the union integrates affirmative action components into its general courses. Apart from specific courses, CUPE puts out several publications that deal with affirmative action, such as an employment equity manual that shows how to prepare an equity plan and an awareness manual that debunks the "ten affirmative action myths".[25]

Enterprise activities in support of affirmative action

That the legislation has resulted in increased equity activities is evidenced by the qualitative measures being undertaken by enterprises as part of their affirmative action plans on behalf of persons with disabilities, (ethnic) visible minorities, as well as women and aboriginal peoples. The following are examples of corporate practices as reported by the enterprises themselves in their annual employment equity reports, as well as in a compendium of enterprise best practices concerning persons with disabilities, published by the Government of Canada.

Canadian National, Canada's national railroad, as part of its community outreach programme, maintains contact with associations representing members of the four designated groups, including having a corporate presence at conferences and workshops that deal with affirmative action issues. This serves to make designated groups aware of the railroad as a potential employer, and provides the company with information on how to facilitate the increased recruitment of designated group members. The railroad also participates as a member of organizations that are dedicated to promote the development of designated groups, such as the Canadian Council on Rehabilitation and Work (for persons with disabilities) and the Centre for Research/Action on Race Relations. Within the company, every internal and external job posting indicates that the railroad is an affirmative action employer that encourages all qualified persons to apply. The company has adopted a policy of modifying the workplace to accommodate employees' needs. As part of National Awareness Week, the railroad invites persons with disabilities to learn about employment with the enterprise. The company has held focus groups with employees to gauge the effectiveness of its equity policies. Finally, a half-day workshop entitled "Managing Diversity" has become a standard part of supervisory training.[26]

The Royal Bank of Canada, one of Canada's largest financial institutions, has established employment equity committees, which include persons with disabilities, (ethnic) visible minorities (as well as women and aboriginal persons) that function in each of its field headquarters. These committees work at the local level towards increasing equity in the bank by running in-house awareness sessions, educational initiatives and outreach activities, and participating in career fairs. Moreover, as part of the field equity activities, the bank has appointed employment equity coordinators at the community level to work with community-based organizations. It also works with organizations such as the Canadian Hearing Society, the Canadian National Institute for the Blind and the Black Cultural Centre to recruit and provide training in order that designated group members might work at the bank or compete for positions on the job market. The field headquarters also sets aside positions for designated group members for temporary and entry-level positions. In terms of other ongoing activities, the bank has implemented a process of interviewing job candidates known as the "behavioural description interviewing technique" which is designed to eliminate systemic barriers to employment faced by designated group members. It provides one-half to one-day employment equity workshops to employees, as well as a one-day "valuing diversity programme" with self-discovery and conflict resolution components.[27]

With reference to equity activities that target persons with disabilities, Bell Canada, a large telecommunications firm, modified its policy to ensure that all new buildings are constructed in accordance with the latest Canadian Standards Association Barrier-Free Design Standard. It also adopted a proactive barrier-free access programme to modify its company buildings to ensure a barrier-free environment for employees, customers and visitors. In the area of job accommodation, decisions about assistive devices and specialized equipment necessary to help employees with disabilities are taken at the departmental level. A company access committee was created to address barriers to employment experienced by persons with disabilities.[28]

Joint review agreements

As noted above, the CHRC will invite employers whose workforce representation of designated groups is low to participate in a joint review of their employment systems. Since the Employment Equity Act's inception, 28 joint reviews have been undertaken.[29]

A good example is the Saskatchewan Wheat Pool, a federally regulated farmers' cooperative. The agreement involves 1,787 employees covering all four designated groups, was approved by the CHRC in April 1992, and is valid until December 1994. It includes an action plan detailing the steps that the Saskatchewan Wheat Pool will undertake to address the equity issues identified by the review process. With reference to persons with disabilities, this joint review determined that the level of representation, based on available 1989 statistics, was between 1.1 per cent and 5.4 per cent of the workforce, depending upon job site and occupational category. Estimates of the availability of disabled workers ranged between 4.1 per cent for middle managers to 10.6 per cent for semi-professional and technical staff. Hiring and promotional goals were set in accordance with these statistics: 8 per cent for clerical staff, 6 per cent for manual workers, 10 per cent for semi-professional and technical staff and 4.1 per cent for middle managers. As for (ethnic) visible minorities, representation ranged from 0 per cent for manual workers to a high of 1.1 per cent for middle and other managers and semi-professional and technical staff. Availability of (ethnic) visible minority workers was determined to be between 1 per cent for skilled construction workers and electricians to 3 per cent for supervisors. Accordingly, hiring and promotional goals reflect attempts to rectify this low representation; the Wheat Pool now seeks to hire, during the review period, between 5 and 6 per cent manual workers, 4 per cent middle managers and between 1 and 2 per cent of various categories of skilled and semi-skilled workers.

The joint review also identified specific changes that would reduce systemic barriers in the Saskatchewan Wheat Pool employment system. For example, there were no clear standards and prescribed processes for the assessment of disabled employment candidates. To rectify this, the enterprise began a physical demands analysis of certain elevator and farm service positions. It also undertook to provide outreach agencies with physical demands profiles, to indicate in job advertisements and postings that such profiles were available and to develop a policy on accommodating the workplace to meet the needs of disabled workers. In addition, negative attitudes were found to exist among a minority of current employees towards designated group individuals in the Province of Saskatchewan. To rectify this, the organization undertook to extend the training workshops it already provides, the aim of which is to sensitize managers and supervisors to the challenges and difficulties that confront persons with disabilities, (ethnic) visible minorities, as well as other designated group members.[30]

    With reference to the impact which joint review activities of the CHRC have had on enterprise behaviour, witnesses, both from employers and organizations representing designated groups to a parliamentary committee that was reviewing the legislation, noted in 1992 that there was a need to evaluate employer compliance. Moreover, employers felt that the proactive consultations of the government equity watchdog agency were important in their achievement of commitment to the principles of employment equity, and that the lack of monitoring and control over employer preparation of employment equity plans was an important obstacle to the proper functioning of the Act.[31]

Empirical studies

    There have been several Canadian studies to determine the effectiveness of the Government's programmes from two dimensions: whether they are having an impact on enterprise behaviour; and whether enterprises are effectively implementing their own affirmative action plans, in order that their own workforce becomes more equitable.

    Leck and Saunders probed the impact of the federal programmes: (1) by examining enterprise commitment to the affirmative action process; (2) by identifying the relationship between affirmative action plans and the attainment of one measure of an equitable workforce representation as evidenced by equitable hiring; and (3) by determining whether or not the presence of an affirmative action plan has a significant impact on the organization's ability to attain a representative workforce over the influence of other factors that affect enterprise behaviour, such as the power and influence of the human resource management department, seniority issues and the business environment.[32] They found that less than half of the organizations surveyed had formalized their affirmative action plans (45 per cent) and set timetables for action (43 per cent). Most surprisingly, they found that 18 per cent of the enterprises surveyed did not have any affirmative action programmes in place, notwithstanding the legal requirement to have such a measure. In addition, only 63 per cent of enterprises integrated their affirmative action plan within the human resource management function by establishing a reporting relationship to an executive level. The authors felt that this had a negative impact on the effectiveness of the affirmative action process and jeopardized the commitment of many enterprises to the affirmative action process.[33] In other words, organizations may not be serious about achieving employment equity and may only be concerned with fulfilling the reporting requirements. In this regard, the legislation itself may be at fault: it fails to state clearly the type and magnitude of expected changes as well as what happens if equity is not achieved.[34]

    Concerning the relationship between affirmative action plans and the attainment of representative hiring, the authors found that three factors — formalization, comprehensiveness and management commitment and support — were the greatest predictors of success. Their research indicated that formalization and comprehensiveness were significantly correlated with the representative hiring of management (ethnic) visible minorities and non-management disabled persons. The reasons why affirmative action plans have differential impact levels on different target groups were unclear: it might be that organizations believe they cannot raise representational levels of all groups every year and therefore concentrate on one or two groups; alternatively, it may be due to the need to put in place different plans to achieve results for different groups.[35]

That the existence of affirmative action plans does have an effect on enterprise behaviour is confirmed by Jain and Hackett, who in 1991 reported their findings concerning the differences between organizations with and without affirmative action programmes. Their study of 648 organizations found that enterprises with plans were more likely to provide recruiter training, ensure that job qualifications were job-related, monitor their staffing practices, furnish gender-neutral documentation, accommodate employees on the basis of religion and collect data concerning the composition of their workforce. However, they reported that only 35 per cent of their respondents were collecting availability data and there was no difference between organizations that had and did not have plans with reference to representation levels. Finally, they found that "a full 50 per cent of our respondents said that they implemented employment equity to improve public relations and as many as 96 per cent claimed that government pressure was a motivating factor".[36]

In 1992 ABT Associates conducted two evaluations for the Government of Canada concerning the Legislated Employment Equity Programme (LEEP) (a form of affirmative action) and the Federal Contractors Programme (FCP). The evaluations concerned, among others, whether programme objectives had been effectively translated into activities and operational goals; and the extent to which the affirmative action programmes have reduced employment inequities faced by members of designated groups.

With reference to the first issue, ABT Associates found that the majority of organizations had not yet incorporated the more significant initiatives into their programmes and, while the LEEP had had a considerable impact on human resource planning, there had been only a limited impact on the budget for human resources and little effect on the employment practices of the organizations. Specifically: 81 per cent had not set goals for promoting designated groups; 86 per cent had not set goals for training designated groups; 51 per cent had not set goals for the hiring of designated groups; while 58 per cent of enterprises had identified systemic barriers to the hiring, training and promotion of designated groups, only 47 per cent had taken actions to eliminate them; and, finally, 80 per cent of enterprises indicated that the affirmative action programmes had very little or no impact on changes to the physical workspace.[37]

On the second issue the results were mixed. For employment growth, their model produced "positive but statistically insignificant coefficients for all the designated groups except women, for whom the sign is negative and not statistically significant". For the hiring of designated groups, "the coefficients for LEEP-covered organizations are negative for all four designated groups, but this is not statistically significant ...". They summarized that "comparable progress was recorded by comparison group organizations. As a result, we are unable to detect positive programme impacts on either employment growth or hires for any of the designated groups". As for representation, all four groups experienced increased levels of representation, but there were large differences. Persons with disabilities and (ethnic) visible minorities attained the greatest positive changes (50 per cent and 33 per cent respectively).[38]

What is most illuminating for this study concerning the impact of affirmative action programmes is ABT Associates' contention that, from a global perspective, the LEEP and the FCP have succeeded in moving employers towards implementing employment equity programmes by creating a social and business climate that is conducive to such changes.

While the existence of the programmes encourages enterprises to embark upon equity activities that might not otherwise take place, actions by the Government to monitor or enforce them yield dramatic increases in the extent of equity activity. The ABT Associates' evaluation of the FCP showed that the compliance review process has had a profound effect on the level of affirmative action initiatives taken by FCP firms. However, it should be pointed out that only 35 per cent of firms have been monitored.[39]

V. BARRIERS TO THE EFFECTIVENESS OF AFFIRMATIVE ACTION PROGRAMMES

It has been demonstrated in this paper that Canada has an increasing number of affirmative action programmes aimed at assisting persons with disabilities and (ethnic) visible minorities to achieve equitable employment, and that these measures have had an impact on the behaviour of enterprises, especially large firms. Yet, in spite of the plethora of programmes in place, members of the designated groups have yet to attain workplace equity. Why is this so?

Answers to this question are not simple. However, it is argued that there are three main barriers to the effectiveness of Canada's affirmative action programmes: continuing overt discrimination; systemic or structural barriers to equitable employment still existent in society; and an incorrect application of affirmative action by many enterprises. In examining these obstacles, it is advanced that the discrimination and systemic barriers experienced by persons with disabilities are fundamentally different from those experienced by (ethnic) visible minorities and, hence, are analysed separately.

(Ethnic) visible minorities

Overt hostile acts of discrimination against (ethnic) visible minorities are difficult to document, due to the social unacceptability of such behaviour. Yet there is ample circumstantial evidence to support the contention that (ethnic) visible minority persons continue to experience discrimination in the workplace and that such discrimination contributes to inequitable employment outcomes, despite the existence of affirmative action programmes. This evidence comes from the results of a survey of employment agencies and the experiences of minority and majority job applicants who tested employers.

A 1987 Canadian Recruiters Guild survey of 672 corporate recruiters, hiring managers and agency recruiters found that 63 per cent admitted to having personal biases against non-whites that have resulted in the rejection of jobseekers; those biased against persons of different national origins were 32 per cent. However, when the percentage of recruiters who reject jobseekers on the basis of past hiring practices within their organizations are included, the discrimination rate is 94 per cent against non-whites and 45 per cent against those of different national origins. This survey also determined that fully 87 per cent of corporate recruiters and 100 per cent of agency recruiters received direct requests to discriminate. These requests were carried out by 73 per cent of corporate recruiters and 94 per cent of those working for an agency.[40]

In 1985, the Social Planning Council of Metropolitan Toronto embarked on a landmark study to determine the extent of racial discrimination in employment by actually sending applicants to apply for positions. Two types of testing were used. In the first, teams of bogus applicants who were professional actors matched as to age, sex, educational and employment qualifications, were sent in person to answer job advertisements listed in a major Toronto newspaper. The types of jobs tested were those that did not require verification or specialized skills, such as sales, retail and the restaurant trade. Applicants all carried résumés that were constructed to meet the requirements of the job being applied for. As for the "candidates", they were chosen to be as alike as possible, the only difference between them being their race. Preferential treatment for whites in the form of differential treatment and actual job offers occurred in nearly one-quarter of cases. The second discrimination test was to find out how job applicants using non-Canadian accents and "ethnic" sounding names would be treated over the telephone. "Over half of the employers practised some form of discrimination against one or more of the callers. The most significant amount of discrimination was directed at the Indo-Pakistanis who were told that jobs were closed or no longer available in 44 per cent of the cases. The black West Indians were told that jobs were closed to them in 36 per cent of the cases. The white immigrant Canadian scored 31 per cent while the white majority Canadians were told that jobs were closed to them in only 13 per cent of the cases tested". The authors concluded that "there is therefore a clear preference by a large proportion of Toronto employers for white employees".[41]

In 1989, Henry repeated her testing. The 1989 testing took place in a labour market characterized by a strong demand for employees and, hence, it was difficult to draw comparisons in terms of the numbers of persons offered employment. However, qualitative indicators pointed to continuing discrimination. "Blacks received worse treatment more often than whites ... the black applicant was likely to be treated badly four times more often than the white applicant".[42] Another example of discrimination was the report's finding that "A pattern which occurred quite frequently was the testing of black applicants ... Accented and non-white job applicants must first prove that they have credentials for the job whereas it is automatically assumed that white applicants have the necessary qualifications ...".[43]

Recently, a series of interviews with (ethnic) visible minority employees of the public service of Canada at the support, officer and management level were conducted. The purpose was to secure these employees' views about their experiences, progress and prospects in the federal public service. It chronicled discrimination, cynicism and lack of confidence in employment practices. Most employees interviewed felt the Government's employment practices were unfair, lacked integrity and were racially biased; such views were also held by persons in management and senior executive positions.[44]

It should be noted, however, that an analysis of complaints received by the CHRC, while indicating a continuing problem of discrimination experienced by (ethnic) visible minorities, may be the basis for optimism: whereas in 1990, discrimination complaints on the grounds of ethnic/national origin, race and colour constituted the largest share received (30 per cent), this figure has continued to decline and amounted in 1993 to 14 per cent.[45]

Structural or systemic barriers continue to have negative impacts on the effectiveness of Canada's affirmative action programmes as they relate to (ethnic) visible minorities. The issues of language training, recognition of academic and professional credentials and barriers in recruitment and selection systems are of the greatest concern.

Until recently, immigrants to Canada who were sponsored by family members, or who were not otherwise oriented to direct labour market entry did not have access to government-run language training. This restriction had a particular impact on immigrant women; one report by the Employment and Immigration Advisory Council found that fully 61 per cent of women were screened out of training as opposed to only 12 per cent of men. This impact on migrant women has resulted in their being held captive in certain low-paying, low status occupations. One of the recommendations made by the report was that "all adult Canadian permanent residents, whether destined for the labour market or not, be they citizens or landed immigrants (regardless of landing date), who have no knowledge of English or French, be eligible for federally funded language training ...".[46] Another obstacle for skilled migrants was the lack of language training that concentrates on professional or trade terminology. Existing government-sponsored language training had placed the accent on communication skills instead of specialized vocabularies needed in certain trades.[47] In response to these criticisms, the Immigration Minister in 1992 implemented new programmes that were open to all, regardless of the participant's labour market intentions. Other new training initiatives now provide specialized labour market oriented training open to those who have a basic knowledge of English or French. As these new measures have yet to be evaluated, it is not known to what extent they will impact on labour market equity for (ethnic) visible minority individuals.[48]

The problem of evaluating the educational and occupational

qualifications of immigrants is a major systemic obstacle to integration into the Canadian labour market. Education is a matter of provincial jurisdiction in Canada; there is no federal ministry. Migrants who wish to practise a trade in Canada must first have their academic qualifications evaluated and a Canadian equivalency determined. In this regard, McDade notes that the appropriate provincial ministry of education assesses the educational qualifications up to the end of secondary school without much difficulty but, beyond this level, "provincial services vary".[49]

Entry into trades also varies from province to province, and depends upon whether the trade is regulated or not. Migrants may not be able to produce documentation attesting to their training. Entry into the professions also presents systemic obstacles for (ethnic) visible minorities. Barriers are due to variations in objectivity, mostly at the level of evaluation of the foreign educational training. While comprehensive evaluating examinations are given in order to assess educational background, such as in pharmacy and medicine, some professions refuse equivalency examinations altogether to graduates of unknown schools.[50]

Recruitment and selection systems also create systemic barriers for the equitable employment of (ethnic) visible minorities. In a study of Toronto employers carried out in 1985, informal recruitment methods were linked to discrimination in employment. The study noted that methods such as word-of-mouth hiring and identification of management potential "in secret" were the most frequent approaches used by organizations to fill vacancies.[51] As recruitment methods are crucial in the development of equitable participation in the workforce, such methods could adversely affect the employment prospects of certain migrants. Selection standards used by employers can also adversely impact on the employment opportunities of migrants and ethnic minorities. Communications skills are rated among the top four selection criteria for management, professional, clerical and sales positions: "Many employers stated that a marked accent, grammatical errors, or a different way of conveying ideas is not considered acceptable for employees in their organizations".[52]

The Billingsley and Muszynski study was carried out before the mandatory federal and many other affirmative action programmes were put in place. In that regard, while a properly implemented affirmative action plan should result in changes in the recruitment and selection systems, the fact remains that the majority of Canadian workers do not fall under the ambit of such programmes. Moreover, as evidence presented in this study indicates, even many employers who are covered by the legislation have a long way to go in implementing changes.

Persons with disabilities

Unlike (ethnic) visible minorities, the discrimination experienced by persons with disabilities is rarely caused by overt hostility. In fact, such discrimination often takes place with the best of intentions and genuine concern about their capabilities and a desire to protect them from harm, injury or embarrassment.[53] Other than these "altruistic" reasons, discrimination faced by persons with disabilities may be based on stereotypical negative attitudes, such as fear that the cost of accommodating persons with disabilities in the workplace is too high, that persons with disabilities are not productive, that other vocational trainees or employees will be uncomfortable in the presence of persons with disabilities and that customers or clients will not be comfortable. Still other attitudes relate to the assumed weakness or sickness of persons with disabilities and the impact this has on their ability to perform the job and/or complete a vocational training programme. The common element is that they are all founded on assumptions based on one characteristic of a person, the presence of a disability.[54]

Such negative attitudes were borne out in two recent studies conducted by Decima Research, a leading Canadian polling organization. In 1992, interviews and focus groups were held with members of the business community, union members and non-workforce participants to gauge their perceptions concerning the integration of persons with disabilities in the workforce. Among the issues raised were the Government's affirmative action measures. It should be noted that these encounters were highly subjective and in no way have been statistically validated. In one study, based on in-depth interviews of business leaders across Canada, from firms of varied size and industrial sector, the cost of accommodating disabled employees was raised by almost one-half of the respondents. Other preoccupations related to lower productivity of disabled persons and feelings that the presence of disabled persons might negatively impact on the image of the firm.[55]

The second study investigated the attitudes of Canadians toward issues related to the integration of disabled persons. Participants felt that disabled persons were as capable and productive as others, but this positive perception was less certain when translated to the participant's own workplace: there was a strong feeling that disabled persons would have "significant" difficulty in performing the job. Factors such as "tight deadlines" or "strong pressures related to the job" were advanced to explain the inability of disabled persons to perform. While there was a consensus about support for the concept of affirmative action, many participants firmly opposed its implementation. Opposition was based on a number of perceptions, such as that it creates resentment, fosters tokenism and goes against the merit principle (there was a clear lack of understanding about the hiring of qualified persons). Participants took exception to the legislative aspect; the idea of being "forced" to hire an individual was seen as still another example of government interference. Moreover, there was absolutely no support for strengthening the programme through the implementation of timetables or quotas.[56]

Persons with disabilities continue to experience structural or systemic barriers. An affirmative action programme may be very well designed, but if the disabled person cannot get to work because the public transportation system is not accessible, or the disabled person cannot enter the place of work because the building doors do not accommodate wheelchairs, or outreach programmes are not in place to address the negative stereotyping and attitudes that persons with disabilities face when seeking employment, or the educational system does not provide the necessary training adapted to the needs of the disabled individual, then the practical outcome is a limitation on the programme's effectiveness.

It appears that there has been an under-utilization of funds available to effect modifications to physical barriers. A general lack of expertise may be one factor to explain this, coupled with the lack of a coordinated approach.[57] A series of reports, entitled "Unequal Access", on accessibility of selected federal offices, telephone services offered by federal departments for hearing-impaired individuals, the availability of government publications in alternative media, the accessibility of banking facilities and postal outlets demonstrates this continuing problem.[58] As for structural barriers in the sense of lower levels of education, the Executive Director of the Canadian Council of Rehabilitation and Work, a bipartite non-governmental organization dedicated to the enhancement of employment opportunities for persons with disabilities, has expressed the view that the ineffectiveness of the affirmative action legislation was not as much the result of the failure to change employers' behaviour as the failure to address other factors that limit the ability of disabled persons to compete effectively, including the lower educational attainment of disabled persons, job accommodation costs for severely disabled individuals, detrimental societal attitudes towards persons with disabilities and disincentives to employment inherent in disability pension programmes.[59]

Apart from the issues of overt discrimination and structural or systemic barriers discussed above, another obstacle to the effective implementation of affirmative action programmes is the failure of the social partners to apply correctly the underlying concepts of affirmative action.

For employers, the lack of understanding of the affirmative action process often manifests itself in preoccupations with mandatory quotas and timetables, as well as a failure to make distinctions between notions of equal and equitable treatment. For example, in the 1992 parliamentary review of the federal Employment Equity Act, employer groups mostly favoured allowing business organizations to determine and establish employment equity plans without the external imposition of quotas, targets or guidelines. Employers cautioned that mandatory numerical goals and timetables would create hostility in the workplace if they replace qualifications as the most important hiring criteria.[60] Employers have also viewed goals and timetables as code words for quotas, and as mentioned above, there is no support for the implementation of quotas.

It is argued that the employer community's preoccupation with setting their own goals and timetables, coupled with the expressed view that replacing qualifications with goals and timetables could cause hostility, and the failure to make clear distinctions between equal and equitable treatment reveal a misunderstanding of the affirmative action process. In fact, goals or quotas are nothing more than objective measures of how well the enterprise is implementing the qualitative changes to the employment system that are the basis of affirmative action — a corporate score-card, as it were. Similarly, it must be recognized that affirmative action is about creating conditions of fairness; it does not mean hiring unqualified persons just to play a numbers game. In this context, the obsession with external goals and statistical reporting is misplaced.

If an enterprise does not fully appreciate the basic tenets of affirmative action, they will not recognize that correctly implementing the affirmative action process results in a more rational utilization of human resources and therefore would have a positive impact on productivity.[61] The end result is, inevitably, a reduced level of commitment, which manifests itself in a failure to undertake the qualitative equity activities needed to ensure success at the enterprise level. For example, the Conference Board of Canada found that a majority of enterprises that participated in their study of affirmative action have not incorporated a system of accountability into their management systems. Accountability is defined as "having some bearing on performance evaluation or compensation" and is seen as being critical in ensuring successful implementation of affirmative action.[62]

The unions have traditionally voiced strong support for affirmative action. However, this support is tempered by the concerns of workers over how they are affected by policies and procedures to combat racism and harassment, viewed by some as forms of "reverse discrimination", and the recognition that the labour movement is not doing enough to confront racism within its own house. Other concerns deal with feelings that the affirmative action process might undermine seniority rights. "What is fair? Who should get the job? How can we reconcile our two competing interests — advancing the rights of members who have been discriminated against and protecting the rights of long-service members? There are no easy answers."[63] The fact that some employees see affirmative action as a threat is also noted by a Conference Board of Canada study that indicated "Only 13 per cent of employment equity officers rated union officials or union representatives as 'very' or 'somewhat' committed (to affirmative action). Forty-two per cent reported that there had been incidence of employee backlash".[64] The extent to which the labour movement is able to confront and rectify resistance caused by misunderstandings of the affirmative action process will greatly affect the pace with which an equitable employment workplace is achieved.

The need, then, for both management and workers to feel an ownership of the affirmative action process is paramount. There have been instances when commitment to affirmative action is articulated at senior levels of the organization. However, if such expressions are not reinforced by activities that result in a "buy-in" to the process at all levels there will not be a change to the enterprise culture that will ensure workplace diversity.[65]

VI. CONCLUSIONS

There is absolutely no question that the enactment of federal affirmative action programmes has been the prime catalyst for enterprises to implement the qualitative changes to their employment systems that will, in the long term, cause changes to enterprise culture resulting, in turn, in a more equitable workplace.[66] More specifically, the evidence adduced in the empirical studies reviewed in this paper indicates that affirmative action programmes do have an impact on the hiring of (ethnic) visible minority persons in both management and non-management positions. Affirmative action plans accounted for variances in the hiring of disabled persons in non-management positions, but did not significantly explain variances in the hiring of disabled persons into management positions. It also emerges that the other specific factor that impacts on the success of affirmative action in any given enterprise is commitment. Without a commitment to the affirmative action process from senior management and employees in general, coupled with managers being held accountable for programme success, there is little chance that an equitable workplace can be achieved.

That said, there is now a division of opinion as to what has been accomplished to date. As noted above, the statistical data show mixed results for both persons with disabilities and (ethnic) visible minorities. Employers take the view that the data are a "benchmark"; that it takes time to review and change employment policies and practices; and that it takes many years to develop people for management and executive positions. Equality-seeking groups, on the other hand, view the slow progress as directly attributable to problems with the legislation; they call for more stringent enforcement measures, including the creation of a separate enforcement agency.[67]

Notwithstanding the divergence of opinion as to how much progress has occurred, the key factor has been that the legislation has placed equality issues in the forefront of public awareness. For example, although only a minority of enterprises are subject to the federal mandatory affirmative action programmes, it is rare indeed to see offers of employment in the newspapers that do not proclaim that "we are an equal opportunity employer", or "our firm is dedicated to employment equity". In this regard, an important aspect of the consciousness building is that the legislation covers not just persons with disabilities or (ethnic) visible minorities, but rather all four categories of persons who have been identified as being disadvantaged, who constitute almost 80 per cent of the Canadian population. This approach encourages the integration of the affirmative action process in a global context of equity and does not create isolated measures in terms of separate programmes and constituencies for the four groups.

To ensure ongoing progress, the equity process must advance beyond its current collection and evaluation of data and the monitoring of employment systems. It is not enough to bring persons with disabilities, (ethnic) visible minorities, aboriginal peoples and women into organizations as they exist now; the organizations must truly change. Organizations must integrate members of designated groups at all levels and, for this to occur, there must be widespread proactive policies that address harassment, discrimination and the accommodation of diversity. The affirmative action process must be integrated into the mainstream of the enterprise, and managers must be held accountable for the successful realization of plans. Since the process of equity is in reality a process of learning, awareness training must take place, not just for employees, but also to sensitize managers. In this regard, enterprises must go beyond cosmetic appearances and begin to implement seriously the qualitative measures that are the backbone of the equity process. It is unacceptable that the vast majority of firms that have been surveyed have not set goals for the recruitment, training and promotion of designated groups, have not taken any steps to eliminate systemic or structural barriers to equitable employment, or have not made their workplaces more physically accessible.

Moreover, government must begin to exercise its enforcement role on a wide front. As noted in the ABT Associates' study of the Federal Contractors Programme, moves by the Government to monitor the process in firms invariably result in increased levels of equity activities. However, the ABT Associates' study also found that only 35 per cent of firms have been monitored and, as of 1991, there were only four Compliance Review Officers who were solely responsible for all compliance cases. Since it has been recognized that very little equity activity takes place in an enterprise without there being a compliance review, one can readily understand the reported frustration over the slow pace of progress.

Finally, it must be understood that employment equity is never finished; it is a process of continuous change and adaptation, the goal of which is the sharing of formerly entrenched power structures in an equitable manner.

Notes

[1] ILO, 1988, p. 177; Employment Equity Act, section 7.

[2] Abella, 1984, pp. 2-3.

[3] Bayefsky and Eberts, 1985, pp. 467-468.

[4] Employment Equity Act, section 4.

[5] ibid., section 3.

[6] Canadian Human Rights Commission, 1992, p. 8; Human Resources Development Canada, 1993, p. 3.

[7] Employment and Immigration Canada, 1986, p. 3.

[8] ibid.; idem, 1991a, p. 2; and 1991b, p. 3.

[9] Canadian Human Rights Commission, 1991a, p. 42.

[10] Employment and Immigration Canada, 1987.

[11] Abella, 1984, pp. 55-97; Roeher Institute, 1992, pp. 5-10, 57; ILO, 1993, pp. 1-2.

[12] Statistics Canada, 1993, p. 5.

[13] Human Resources Development Canada, 1993, pp. 37-39.

[14] ibid., p. 4.

[15] ibid., p. 39.

[16] Roeher Institute, 1992, p. 9.

[17] Human Resources Development Canada, 1993, pp. 44-45.

[18] ibid., p. 46.

[19] Samuel, 1989-90.

[20] Raskin, 1993, p. 54.

[21] Redway, 1992, pp. 31-32.

[22] Canadian Advisory Council on the Status of Women, 1992, p. 22; Rebick and Poole, 1992, pp. 6-7.

[23] Labine, 1994.

[24] Onyalo, 1994.

[25] Howell, 1994.

[26] Canadian National Railways Company, 1993, pp. 1-3.

[27] Royal Bank of Canada, 1993, pp. 1-4; White, L., 1994.

[28] Treasury Board of Canada, 1993, pp. 52-83.

[29] Canadian Human Rights Commission, 1992a, p. 7; Redway, 1992, p. 25; Phillips, 1992-94.

[30] Canadian Human Rights Commission and Saskatchewan Wheat Pool, 1992.

[31] Redway, 1992, p. 26; Tellier, 1994.

[32] Leck and Saunders, 1991, pp. 8-11.

[33] ibid., pp. 12-17.

[34] ibid., pp. 16-17, 25.

[35] ibid., pp. 17-21.

[36] Jain and Hackett, 1991, pp. 8-9.

[37] ABT Associates, 1992b, pp. 22-24.

[38] ibid., pp. 36, 40.

[39] idem, 1992a, pp. 1, 8, 18, 20, 37, 46.

[40] Canadian Recruiters Guild, 1987.

[41] Henry and Ginzberg, 1985, pp. 4-5.

[42] Henry, 1989, pp. 22-23.

[43] ibid., p. 24.

[44] Treasury Board of Canada, 1993, pp. 2-3.

[45] Canadian Human Rights Commission, 1994, p. 56.

[46] Employment and Immigration Advisory Council, 1991, p. 56.

[47] McDade, 1988, p. 11.

[48] Employment and Immigration Canada, 1991c, pp. 2-4; idem, 1992; Holmes, 1994.

[49] McDade, 1988, p. 27.

[50] ibid., p. 12.

[51] Billingsley and Muszynski, 1985, pp. 17-23.

[52] ibid., p. 25.

[53] Molloy, 1992, p. 26.

[54] Roeher Institute, 1992, pp. 5-10, 57; Ontario Advisory Council for Disabled Persons, 1990, p. 105.

[55] Decima Research, 1992b, pp. 7-22.

[56] idem, 1992a, pp. 3, 15-21.

[57] OECD, 1992, p. 30.

[58] Canadian Human Rights Commission, 1990, 1991b, 1991c, 1992b, 1992c.

[59] McInnes, 1992, pp. 11:21-11:22.

[60] Employment and Immigration Canada, 1991d, p. 19.

[61] Jain and Hackett, 1991, p. 7.

[62] Benimadhu and Wright, 1992, p. 16.

[63] Howell, 1994; White, R., 1994, p. 2.

[64] Benimadhu and Wright, 1992, pp. 14-15.

[65] ibid., p. 16.

[66] ibid., p. 12.

[67] ibid., p. 5; Redway, 1992, p. 26.

INDIA
Amajeet Kaur*

2

I. PERSONS WITH DISABILITIES

Definitions of physical disability

Despite a breakthrough in health services in India, a number of disabilities continue to appear due to polio, communicable and congenital diseases, increased industrialization and mechanization, vehicular traffic leading to locomotor disabilities; there are also vitamin A deficiency, cataract and infectious injuries and nutritional deficiency leading to visual loss, as well as ear infections, external injuries and noise pollution contributing to hearing loss.

The Government is providing a large number of facilities and concessions to disabled persons. In order to provide these facilities and concessions, it was imperative that a standard definition of these disabilities be decided upon. Following a recommendation of the National Council for Handicapped Welfare, a committee recommended adopting this classification:

(a) Impairment: An impairment is a permanent or transitory psychological or anatomical loss and/or abnormality, such as an amputated limb, paralysis after polio, myocardial infarction, cerebrovascular thrombosis, restricted pulmonary capacity, diabetes, myopia, disfigurement, mental retardation, hypertension, perceptual disturbance.

(b) Functional limitations: Impairment may cause functional limitations which are the partial or total inability to perform those activities necessary for motor, sensory or mental functions within the range and manner of which a human being is normally capable, such as walking, lifting loads, seeing, speaking, hearing, reading, writing, counting, taking interest in and making contact with surroundings. A functional limitation may last for a short time, a long time, be permanent or reversible.

---

* World Federation of Trade Unions.

(c)   Disability: Disability is defined as an existing difficulty in performing one or more activities which, in accordance with the subject's sex and social role, are generally accepted as essential basic components of daily living such as self-care, social relations and economic activity. Depending in part on the duration of the functional limitation, a disability may be short term, long term or permanent.

Medically, disability is physical impairment and inability to perform physical functions normally. Legally, disability is a permanent injury to the body for which the person should or should not be compensated. Both of these concepts apply when looking at the employment of persons with disabilities.

According to the National Sample Survey, conducted in 1991, there are 14.56 million persons suffering from physical disability — these constitute 1.9 per cent of the total population of the country. The results of the survey on mentally retarded persons are not yet published. However, various studies conducted by research organizations show that about 3 per cent of the population suffer from mental retardation. The real number of disabled persons is about 50 million, 45 per cent of whom suffer an extreme degree of disability, cannot be employed or self-employed and need to be looked after by the Government and community.

Overview of the historical aspects

Voluntary organizations were formed in the mid-1940s at the initiative of social workers for the welfare of disabled persons. With the passing of time, awareness grew and pressure was exerted on the Government, resulting in it taking up the issue of funding welfare schemes for them. Non-governmental organizations (NGOs) and voluntary social groups played a big role in heightening community awareness to their cause and the disabled persons themselves also played a vital role in the campaigns, programmes and militant actions to bring the point home.

NGOs asserted that persons with disabilities needed training and pushed for the rapid establishment of the institutes for such purposes. Once the process started, some such institutions were established by the Government and some independent efforts were also supported by government funds. Then followed the question of the fruitful employment of these persons. The motivation came from groups of disabled persons themselves, who insisted that the Government reserve certain jobs for disabled persons. An initial Office Memorandum, issued by the Ministry of Home Affairs in 1961, gave concessions to the physically handicapped with regard to qualifications for typing speed for appointments in lower division clerical posts. But there was no reservation of posts, so this attempt at affirmative action did not succeed. In the 1970s, the movement for job reservations gained momentum. In 1977 the Government issued a second Office Memorandum announcing reservations in the less senior categories of the central Government (groups C and D) for disabled persons as follows:

—	the blind	1 per cent
—	the deaf	1 per cent
—	orthopaedics	1 per cent

For certain government positions it is stipulated that persons beyond a set maximum age cannot apply; the specific age is job and category dependent. However, the Government has instituted a policy by which persons with disabilities may apply for a position up to ten years beyond the maximum age applicable to non-disabled applicants (Order No. 15012/6/77 of 28 January 1978). Moreover, a conveyance (travel) allowance was instituted on 31 August 1978. However, there was no serious action taken by the ministries themselves to implement the orders of the Ministry of Home Affairs. Vacant positions posted at employment exchanges that were supposed to indicate that they were reserved for disabled persons or other reserved categories did not do so (Office Memorandum No. 14016/3/78 dated 21 May 1979). In addition, the private sector, while not covered under the quota programme, was not heeding the Government's appeals to hire these persons. The lack of implementation by the Government's own ministries was stressed in two later Office Memoranda (No. 39016/24/80 of 1 December 1980 and No. 1801/1/80 dated 27 June 1980), particularly in relation to the employment of blind persons.

It was only in 1980 that yearly marking of jobs for handicapped persons was ordered to be prepared by government offices. Finally, in 1984 the Government set up a committee to examine the entire question of the place of persons with disabilities in employment. It identified 1,100 out of 3,000 positions listed in the classification of occupations as being suitable for filling by such people. It should be noted that groups representing persons with disabilities were not represented on the committee. It was not until an Office Memorandum of 1986 that the actual details of the identified jobs became available.

Despite all these measures, prejudices against the disabled in the field of employment continued. Office Memorandum No. 36035/5/85 dated 25 July 1985 notes that:

> On the basis of returns received in the Ministry of Social and Women's Welfare, it has been observed that there has not been any significant progress in the implementation of the reservation orders in respect of all categories of the handicapped, and the category of the blind in particular; resulting in disillusionment among them, particularly in the latter. It has also been brought to the Government's notice that certain traditional prejudices still persist among some of the employing authorities who perhaps labour under the impression that the handicapped persons are necessarily less productive than the able-bodied. This is not always borne out by studies in this regard. Given the requisite technological support in the posts that have been identified to be fit to be held by handicapped persons, they have proved themselves equal to the job requirements. There has therefore to be a change in attitude towards this handicapped section of society which reassures and generates confidence in them. All ministries/departments are, therefore, requested to impress upon all the appointing authorities to rise above such prejudices, if any, and ensure employment of blind persons against identified reserved vacancies in the public services.

Some improvement followed this exhortation: persons who apply to sit the competitive examinations for staff selection, or who otherwise apply for a position in government, must pay an application fee, but this fee has been waived for persons with disabilities (Office Memorandum No. 39022/1/85).

The question of promotion was taken up only some years later, in Office Memorandum No. 36035/8/89 dated 20 November 1989. According to this text, reservations in promotions will be provided to physically handicapped persons within the less senior central government staff categories (services C and D).

Another committee was formed in 1986 to study the identification of jobs in the senior staff groups for disabled persons; it identified 420 jobs indicating which ones could be held by each category of such people. It noted one particular obstacle in the appointment of disabled persons to the central government services in certain organized services: recruitment is made at the lowest level and the higher posts are filled by promotion; a person recruited at the lowest level cannot be ignored for promotion to the higher posts in the same service, provided the prescribed period of experience has been completed. However, in many services, the nature of duties to be performed at one level are substantially different from the nature of duties at a different level, and the medical examination completed upon initial recruitment which is adapted for the quota of handicapped persons might mean that the handicapped employee is promoted irrespective of the physical requirements of the new job. Fear of this occurring is one of the main constraints restricting recruitment of handicapped persons to the organized services. The committee, however, recommended that there should be no bar in considering handicapped persons for recruitment to such services, on the clear understanding that they would be promoted only up to a certain level.

The committee also observed a paradoxical situation to the effect that while handicapped persons were demanding more and more jobs in wider areas of occupation, public sector and government departments did not get an adequate number of sponsored candidates for various jobs, apparently due to the non-availability of properly trained handicapped persons. The committee therefore recommended that the Ministry of Labour reiterate its instructions to employment exchanges and vocational rehabilitation centres so that when suitable handicapped persons are not available for a particular job, the central employment exchange advertise such jobs through newspapers, radio and TV to reach out to the largest possible pool of qualified handicapped candidates.

Another comment of the committee was that the task of identification of jobs is an ongoing one. With new technologies, new kinds of jobs are being created and in such cases the various ministries and departments should refer the job description of such new types of jobs to the committee so as to enable it to consider the suitability of such jobs for physically handicapped persons. It was agreed that the committee would also review its own identification of jobs at regular intervals.

Despite all these efforts undertaken by the committee, the Government still did not decide to reserve posts in the senior categories of government staff. There was and continues to be general resistance by the various ministries and departments to considering disabled persons for such jobs.

Affirmative action by the Government

Article 46 of the Constitution enjoins the State to promote with special care the educational and economic interests of the "weaker sections" of the people. Although there is no specific mention of disabled persons, the term "weaker sections" would seem to cover them.

According to entry 9 in List II of Schedule 7 of the Constitution, the subject of "relief to the disabled and unemployable" is the responsibility of the state governments. Despite this, in practice the central Government plays a major role in administrative arrangements. The Ministry of Welfare has been identified as the nodal ministry and all policy initiatives in this area are taken by it. Some of the programmes are implemented through non-government organizations and monitored through the state governments.

In consonance with the policy of providing a complete package of welfare services to physically and mentally handicapped individuals and groups and in order to deal effectively with the multidimensional problems facing them, the following national institutes have been set up in each major area of disability: (1) the National Institute for the Visually Handicapped, Dehradun; (2) the National Institute for the Orthopaedically Handicapped, Calcutta; (3) the Ali Yavar Jung National Institute for the Hearing Handicapped, Bombay; and (4) the National Institute for the Mentally Handicapped, Secunderabad.

These institutes are apex-level organizations in the field of education, training, vocational guidance, counselling, research, rehabilitation and development of suitable service modules for the handicapped. They also serve as documentation and information centres in their respective areas of disability. Development and standardization of aids and appliances and preparation of community awareness materials, both for the electronic and the print media and for the target audience, be they parents, the community and professionals working in the field, and so on, are not their responsibilities.

In addition to the four national institutes, the following two organizations have been working in the field to provide training facilities and services for rehabilitation of persons with locomotor disabilities: the Institute for the Physically Handicapped (IPH) in New Delhi and the National Institute of Rehabilitation, Training and Research (NIRTAR) in Orissa.

The Artificial Limbs Manufacturing Corporation (ALIMCO), Kanpur, was established as a public sector company with the main objective of developing and manufacturing standard aids and appliances for disabled persons and to make them available at reasonable prices throughout India. In 1981, the Scheme of Assistance to Disabled Persons for the Purchase and Fitting of Aids and Appliances was also entrusted to ALIMCO for implementation.

The Government of India has also set up the Rehabilitation Council of India to enforce uniform standards in training of professionals in the field of rehabilitation for the handicapped, maintenance of the Central Rehabilitation Register and other connected matters. The Rehabilitation Council of India Act came into force on 31 July 1993.

With a view to providing suitable and cost-effective aids and appliances through the application of technology and also to improving the mobility, employment opportunities and integration of the disabled into mainstream employment, the "Science and Technology Project in Mission Mode" was launched in 1988. Suitable research and development projects are identified and funded (on a 100 per cent basis) under the scheme. So far, 45 projects have been identified for assistance and about 37 of them are moving towards completion. Some of them have led to commercial production. Products like computerized Braille embossers, speech synthesizers, feeding aids for spastic children, interpointing Braille writing frames, electronic guide sticks and photovoltaic battery chargers have been developed under the project.

The various special measures described above are, however, only ancillary to the affirmative action taken in favour of employment of handicapped persons. There are general employment exchanges in all the states and union territories of India. Out of all these employment exchanges, 55 have been given grants by the Government to operate special sections (known as cells) that are concerned only with the employment of persons with disabilities. But what is the situation in reality with regard to this structure to facilitate entry or re-entry into employment? The figures show that total placements of disabled persons in jobs have been 50,000 between 1959 and 1994. This figure includes those in government jobs and in the private sector. As there is not much scope of employment in the government and private sectors, efforts are at present urgently needed in promoting self-employment. For that, the existing banking loan provisions are no help at all, and serious programming is needed in this respect.

To provide recognition by the State of the rights of persons with disabilities to enjoy equality of opportunity and full participation in national life, the Ministry of Welfare drafted new legislation: the Persons with Disabilities (Securities and Rehabilitation) Bill, 1994. The proposed legislation covered areas like the creation of central and state coordination committees, prevention, early detection, intervention, education, employment and vocational training, non-discrimination, etc. This draft Bill has been circulated to different ministries for their comments and suggestions.

With the adoption, on 1 January 1996, of the Persons with Disabilities (Equal Opportunities, Protection of Rights and Full Participation) Act (No. 1 of 1996), the Government has finally committed itself to moving ahead in most of these areas. There is to be a Central Coordination Committee, with a broad composition including representatives of disability NGOs, to serve as the national focal point on disability matters and advise the central Government. Every state shall have such a committee. The reservation of 3 per cent of public posts shall continue and all educational institutions receiving government aid shall reserve not less than 3 per cent of places for persons with disabilities. Chapter VII of the Act deals with affirmative action through preferential allotment of land for, inter alia, setting up businesses and establishing factories by entrepreneurs with disabilities. The Chief Disability Commissioner and State Committees have power to enforce the non-discrimination provisions of the new Act and monitor the utilization of funds, with the Chief Commissioner's annual report to be tabled in Parliament. It will be interesting to see how these provisions are put into practice.

Current situation and conclusions

The National Council for Handicapped Welfare met in September 1994 in New Delhi with the participation of ministers from state governments, different relevant departments and heads of some NGOs, all of whom are members of the Council. Of its many recommendations, the most relevant for this study are:

1. Given that the draft legislation "Persons with Disabilities (Security and Rehabilitation) Bill, 1994" was generally supported, an intensive effort had to be made to arrive at a general consensus on the Bill before it was introduced in Parliament. Now that the 1996 Act is law, it will be vital that the consensus on its usefulness continues to boost its acceptance in practice.

2. The scale of assistance to voluntary organizations should be increased. The scheme could then provide central government funds to agencies for release of grant-in-aid directly to voluntary organizations by the concerned states or union territories.

3. All state governments or union territories should make efforts to formulate policies for handicapped welfare. A national policy for handicapped welfare may be formulated by the Ministry of Welfare. Under the new law, the Central or State Coordination Committees will have this function.

4. The National Handicapped Finance and Development Commission should be constituted as early as possible.

5. Three per cent reservation of jobs should be uniformly provided in the state governments' or union territories' administration and strict implementation of the reservation percentage should be ensured.

6. Reservation of jobs for the disabled should be encouraged in the private sector also with provision for suitable incentives to encourage employers to undertake such reservations.

7. The District Rehabilitation Centres Scheme should be expanded to serve as a focal point at the district level for providing rehabilitation services to rural disabled persons. The scheme should be modified to encourage NGOs to undertake district level rehabilitation schemes.

8. The condition of two years of existence of voluntary organizations for eligibility for grant-in-aid should be relaxed in appropriate cases.

9. Regional centres of National Institutes should be set up in order to extend the outreach of interdisciplinary facilities for technical guidance to the voluntary organizations for disabled persons.

10. The scholarship scheme should be handed back to the central administration as the state governments find it difficult to muster enough resources for the provision of scholarships.

11. The subject of disability should be transferred from the list of responsibilities vested solely in the states to the concurrent list.

12. Aids and appliances should be supplied to the disabled in a time-bound manner and the condition of supply of certain parts by ALIMCO should be considered for relaxation.

13. A central agency should be formed for establishing and managing special schools.

The deliberations were indicative of the poor implementation of the existing schemes, as well as the employment situation. Now that there is new, comprehensive federal legislation establishing the machinery for a national policy for handicapped welfare, it is hoped that its implementation will be taken seriously.

It was pointed out by many during interviews for this chapter that India, being a developing country with 50 million persons with disabilities, cannot cope with the problems of disabled persons having varying degrees of handicap through community services alone. The State has to bear the responsibility.

The courts are playing a role in supporting mainstream employment in this area. Following the favourable judgements of the Supreme Court of India, the Madras High Court and the Patna High Court in three separate cases concerning persons with disabilities, there is more awareness among the educated and leading disabled activists, and they are more confident in putting forth their demands. The Supreme Court case examined the refusal in the central administrative services to allow the blind to sit competitive examinations, and upheld the plea of the blind candidate that blindness in no way hinders the person from doing administrative jobs. In the Madras case, a blind person won the case of being capable of handling the job of principal in a high school. In the third case, another blind person won by proving that he was able to conduct the job as a member of the State Public Service Commission.

The passage of the Persons with Disabilities (Equal Opportunities, Protection of Rights and Full Participation) Act in 1996 demonstrates the Government's commitment to eliminating employment discrimination against disabled persons. The legislation, which largely adopted the demands of disabled persons, their representatives, academics and the sensitized sections of society, indicates both a sensitivity to the problems confronting the disabled as well as the political will to act. It remains to be seen how the Act will be applied in practice.

II. "ETHNIC" MINORITIES

The concept of ethnicity in the Indian context

Documents dating back to the fourteenth century AD identified one original grouping, called the "Jatis". The Jatis were a local institution, having their own local traditions, language and culture.

In the colonial period, the concept of ethnography as we understand it today emerged, due to colonial needs for information in the commercial and economic spheres. The listing of castes started in 1806 and gained momentum in the censuses of the period 1871 to 1931 when religion and language were also included in census data.

The term "caste" has been in use for the last 400 years and the term "nationality" for the last 75 years, whereas the term "ethnicity" has been increasingly used over the last 35 years or so. While caste is not an ethnic category, it is sometimes described as a gene pool. Nationality has been defined by language. During the struggle for independence from colonial rule, the leaders promised to reorganize the states on the basis of language. Thus, in the mid-1950s, the process of organization of the country on the basis of the major language or the scheduled language in the Constitution began. It was completed with the formation of Punjab State in 1966. The Constitution of India, in its Eighth Schedule, lists the languages to be officially used by the State or central Government for the purposes of education, communication, administration, and so on. Thus, the Constitution takes into account diversities, particularly those based on regions and languages, but not the concept of ethnicity as such. It recognizes five social categories: (1) the Scheduled Castes; (2) the Scheduled Tribes; (3) Anglo-Indians; (4) backward classes; and (5) religious and linguistic minorities. None of these (with the possible exception of some sections of the tribes and Anglo-Indians) could be considered "ethnic" in the traditional sense of the term.

In 1985 a government survey identified 4,635 "ethnic" communities throughout India. It described the relationship of castes and sub-castes, of tribes and sub-tribes, of communities with one another in local and regional contexts. According to this survey the total number of synonyms, titles, subgroups, and so on, stands at 60,000.

Affirmative action in employment

The Constitution (article 16) guarantees equality of opportunity for all citizens in matters relating to employment or appointment to any office under the State, and article 16(4) states that: "Nothing in this article shall prevent the State from making any provision for the reservation of appointments or posts in favour of any backward class or citizen which, in the opinion of the State, is not adequately represented in the services under the State."

This provision was used by the State to issue Ordinances and Office Memoranda and to enact legislation for positive measures in favour of the Scheduled Castes and Tribes. These published lists may be reviewed from time to time for exclusion or inclusion of a caste or tribe. The determination of "backward classes" is left to the State, to act according to the advice of the Backward Classes Commission (formed under article 340 of the Constitution).

According to the jurisprudence of the Supreme Court of India, two conditions are necessary for scheduling: a class of citizens who are backward, socially and educationally; and the said class is not adequately represented in the services under the State. Economic conditions and occupations were the factors to be taken into consideration in determining social backwardness; caste may also be a relevant consideration but could not be the sole or dominant test for this purpose. Though Scheduled Castes and Tribes are not separately mentioned in article 16(4), it has been held that they are entitled to be treated as "backward" classes and that accordingly, any reservation or relaxation of service conditions for appointment or promotion cannot be challenged as discriminatory, provided such reservation is not excessive. There is a limit of 50 per cent for reservation under the latest rulings of the Supreme Court.

Articles 341 and 342 of the Constitution define who may be included in Scheduled Castes (SCs) and Scheduled Tribes (STs), with respect to any state or union territory. Interstate area restrictions have been imposed so that only the people belonging to the specific community residing in the specific area, which has been assessed to qualify for listing as an SC or ST, benefit from the facilities provided for them.

Affirmative action for the SCs and STs commenced with the attainment of independence, when instructions were issued in September 1947 providing for the reservation of 12.5 per cent of central government service vacancies for SCs in respect of recruitment made by open competition. In the case of recruitment otherwise than by competition, this percentage was fixed at 16.67 per cent. After the Constitution was promulgated, Government Resolution of 13 September 1950 set a 5 per cent reservation of STs apart from the percentage already fixed for SCs. The 1961 census revealed that the SC and ST population in proportion to the Indian population stood at 14.64 per cent and 6.8 per cent respectively. Accordingly, the percentage of reservations for SCs and STs was increased from 12.5 per cent and 5 per cent to 15 per cent and 7.5 per cent respectively on 25 March 1970.

Reservations have been extended to other modes of promotion in stages. In 1957, reservations were provided for SCs and STs in departmental competitive examinations. Reservation for promotion numbers was commenced in 1963, and in the same year, reservation in departmental competitive examination was limited to certain public service grades. The position was slightly changed in 1968, when reservation in limited departmental examinations and promotion by selection to certain senior classes were subject to the condition that direct recruitment should not exceed 50 per cent. Reservation for the number of promotions by seniority subject to fitness came in 1972, on condition that the element of direct recruitment does not exceed 50 per cent. The limitation of 50 per cent was raised to 66.67 per cent in 1976.

The rule regarding carrying forward of unfilled reserved posts has also undergone changes over the years. In 1952, the unfilled reserved vacancies for SCs and STs were required to be carried forward to one subsequent recruitment year; in 1955 to two subsequent recruitment years; and in 1970 to three subsequent recruitment years (except in certain promotions by selection where the principle of carry forward does not apply). Along with the principle of carrying forward, there is provision for the exchange of vacancies between SCs and STs.

However, although the Constitution provides for the appointment by the Government of special officers (article 338) to verify that the affirmative action programmes to benefit the SCs and STs are implemented, it was clear that developments were not moving as desired. In 1978, the Government set up a commission for the SCs and STs within the Ministry of Home Affairs (Resolution No. 13013/9/77-SCT(I) of 21 July 1978). The commission's annual reports to the President of India time and again brought the truth to the forefront: the government policies were not being implemented and discrimination continued (only 5 per cent representation had been attained for SCs in Class I posts as against a quota of 15 per cent and the representation of STs in Class I posts was only 1.04 per cent as against a quota of 7.5 per cent). The welfare schemes were also not having the desired results for the recipients.

This state of affairs resulted in a constitutional amendment, which came into effect on 12 March 1992, aimed at giving the commission — composed of a chairperson, vice-chairperson and five other members — statutory powers. It is to investigate and monitor all matters relating to the affirmative action measures provided for the SCs and STs, participate and advise in the planning process for their socio-economic development, discharge such other functions in relation to the protection, welfare development and advancement of the SCs and STs and to make such reports and recommendations as to steps that should be taken by the Union or the states for effective implementation of the measures. It is mandatory for the central and state governments to consult the commission in respect of any policy measures affecting the SCs and STs. The commission has also been vested with the powers of a civil court examining a suit. The first report of this national commission is yet to be tabled in Parliament.

A different form of affirmative action was required for the backward classes who, contrary to the SCs and STs which enjoyed job reservations from 1950 onwards, benefitted from no such provisions. Moves for this began in the 1970s, and led to the appointment of a commission by the central Government to study this question. This commission, known as the Mandal Commission after its chairperson, published its categorization of other backward castes in 1977. Its report was discussed in Parliament in

1982 and 1983 and action was taken by the Government in the form of a Memorandum, issued on 13 August 1990, reserving 27 per cent of government post vacancies for the "socially and educationally backward classes" (SEBCs). A second Memorandum was issued on 25 September 1991 amending the first so as to allow preference to be given to candidates from the poorer sections of the SEBCs. There has been controversy over the question of job reservations for the SEBCs, but the Supreme Court has upheld the constitutionality of the 27 per cent reservation, subject to the exclusion of the socially advanced persons (described as the "creamy layer") (*Indira Sowtney and others v. Union of India and others*, 16 November 1992).

There are no provisions in the Constitution regarding the employment of religious or linguistic minorities, nor is there any provision for affirmative action programmes for that purpose. Under the Constitution, articles 14 and 15 guarantee the absence of discrimination on grounds of religion and language and, therefore, the rights of individual members or religious and linguistic minorities are secured in common with those of other citizens. The linguistic minorities have been provided with special constitutional safeguards under articles 347, 350 and 350A, and article 350B provides for the appointment of a special officer for linguistic minorities to ensure that the safeguards provided to them in the Constitution are observed. A Minorities Commission was set up by the Government (Resolution No. II-16012/2/77-NID(D) dated 12 January 1978); however, it was amended by Resolution No. IV.12011/2/88-CLM of 30 March 1988 to provide that the Minorities Commission would be concerned with safeguarding the interests of minorities based on religion only and the special officer appointed under the above-mentioned article 350B (commonly known as the Commissioner for Linguistic Minorities) would not function as secretary of the Commission, as had been originally envisaged. The Minorities Commission has no statutory power and plays a merely advisory role. Its first report is yet to be placed before Parliament.

As explained above, the Constitution provides for the safeguarding and development of SCs and STs, groups which had suffered social discrimination, economic deprivation and educational backwardness. The Government has therefore initiated a number of measures relating to: (1) protection, as enshrined in the Constitution and enactments by legislation; (2) development, by providing economic benefits through various schemes and programmes; and (3) affirmative action programmes in education and employment facilities. Special efforts are made through the Special Component Plan for SCs, the Special Central Assistance Body, and the creation of SCs' development corporations to accelerate the economic development of this marginalized group.

According to the 1991 census, the population of SCs represents 16.48 per cent of the total population. The Ministry of Welfare acts as the coordinator of the various welfare activities for the SCs and monitors the special component plans of all the states and territories and the ministries and departments of the central Government. In addition, the Ministry has its own central and centrally sponsored schemes and programmes implemented through state governments and territory administrations and various NGOs for the social, educational and economic development of the SCs. It is recognized by the Ministry that the major problems faced by SCs' development continue to be economic, educational and social. There is a vital need for special attention to be given to groups like landless labourers, marginal farmers, artisans, civic sanitation workers, flayers, tanners and leatherworkers and other unorganized labourers.

Some innovations have been: the creation in 1989 of the National Scheduled Castes and Scheduled Tribes Finance and Development Corporation (NSFDC), a non-profit company, which plays a catalytic role in development schemes for employment generation for SCs and STs; SCs' development corporations (currently 18 in states and four in union territories); national overseas scholarships and passage grants for higher studies abroad; aid to voluntary organizations for SCs (technical training is given to enable them to engage in income-generating activities for economic development); grant-in-aid provided directly to the voluntary organizations who are engaged in extending such facilities to SCs; the National Scheme of Liberation and Rehabilitation of Scavengers (to provide alternative dignified and viable trades and occupations to scavengers and their dependants for five-year periods); research and training relating to SCs' development (financial assistance given to universities, organizations and research institutions which have proven expertise and are willing to undertake purposeful studies to evaluate the economic development, problems and requirements of SCs); post-secondary-school scholarships for SC and ST students (payment of all tuition and compulsory fees as well as a maintenance allowance); pre-matriculation scholarships for the children of those engaged in unclean occupations started in 1977-78, with central government assistance provided to the state governments on a 50:50 basis); book banks for SC and ST students; hostels for girls and boys from SCs; and coaching schemes (central government financial assistance is provided for coaching to candidates through pre-examination recruitment training centres to improve their representation in various services in the central and state governments and public undertakings).

STs form 8.08 per cent of the country's total population according to the 1991 census. The above-mentioned constitutional articles which have a direct bearing on the development of STs are 15(4), 16(4), 19(5), 46, 164, 244, 275(i), 330, 332, 334, 338, 339, 342 and the Fifth and Sixth Schedules.

Although literacy is one of the key inputs for socio-economic development, the STs lag behind others in this field, specifically in the case of females. According to the 1991 census, female literacy among STs was 8.05 per cent. There are 48 districts in eight states with tribal concentration where literacy of female tribals is less than 2 per cent.

The strategy for development of STs is primarily based on the Tribal Sub-Plan approach. It has two objectives: protective measures for the elimination of exploitation through legal support and improving the level of administration of tribal areas; and promotion of development efforts through schemes to raise the standard of living. The Tribal Sub-Plan has been in operation since 1974-75 in 18 states and two union territories and is being implemented through 193 integrated tribal development projects, 249 modified area development approach pockets and 77 clusters of tribal concentration, and through micro-projects for 74 primitive tribal groups.

Paragraph 3 of the Fifth Schedule to the Constitution requires the Governor of each state having scheduled areas to make a report to the President annually regarding administration of scheduled areas (scheduled areas have been declared in eight states). Moreover, according to paragraph 4 of the Fifth Schedule, each state having a scheduled area should create a Tribal Advisory Council, which has a role to play in employment advice.

Further ventures include: a scheme of boys' and girls' hostels for members of STs; a new scheme of educational complexes in low literacy areas for the development of female tribals' literacy as of 1993-94; the Tribal Cooperative Marketing Development Federation of India Limited (TRIFED) (set up by the central Government in August 1987 with an authorized share capital of Rs.20.00 crores); grant-in-aid to state tribal development cooperative corporations for minor forest produce operations; a scheme of grant-in-aid to voluntary organizations working for the welfare of STs; and research and training. For research and training, financial assistance is given to the state governments and NGOs in three different forms: grants in favour of tribal research institutes on a 50:50 basis; fellowships to students who are registered in a university on a 100 per cent basis; and grants to institutes and organizations for conducting research and evaluation studies on a 100 per cent basis; there are 14 tribal research institutes in the States of Andhra Pradesh, Assam, Gujarat, Kerala, Madhya Pradesh, Maharashtra, Orissa, Rajasthan, Tamil Nadu, West Bengal, Uttar Pradesh, Manipur and Tripura.

The above-mentioned central government Memoranda of 13 August 1990 and 25 September 1991 provide for the reservation of civil service posts for socially and educationally backward classes and other economically backward sections not already covered by the existing reservation schemes. Following the Supreme Court's validation of this reservation, the central Government, as well as the governments of the states and the union territories, have set about specifying the bases for excluding the "creamy layer" from the other backward classes. The Government set up an expert committee in February 1993 to recommend the socio-economic criteria for identification of the "creamy layer": the exclusion will apply to the son(s) and daughter(s) of: persons holding constitutional positions like the President of India, Vice-President of India, judges of the Supreme Court and high courts, chairperson and members of the Public Service Commissions; of parents holding high civil service or military posts; and of families owning large areas of irrigated land or having substantial gross annual incomes. The committee's report, which was accepted by the Government, was tabled in Parliament on 16 March 1993. An amended Memorandum, to replace that of 13 August 1990, was issued on 8 September 1993 providing for reservation of 27 per cent of the vacancies in civil service posts under the central Government for the other backward classes, subject to the exclusion of the "creamy layer". The Government has subsequently notified the lists of other backward classes in respect of 14 States (Assam, Andhra Pradesh, Bihar, Goa, Gujarat, Haryana, Himachal Pradesh, Karnataka, Kerala, Maharashtra, Madhya Pradesh, Punjab, Tamil Nadu and Uttar Pradesh) which together account for 80 per cent of the country's population. Subsequently, the States of Rajasthan, Orissa, and Sikkim have also submitted their lists.

The National Commission for Backward Classes Act, 1993, has been enacted to provide for the setting-up of a permanent body at the national level to recommend the inclusion and/or exclusion of any caste or community from the list of other backward classes, whose recommendations would be binding on the Government. The National Commission was set up on 14 August 1993. There is also a National Backward Classes Finance and Development Corporation, set up on 13 January 1992 (similar to that created in 1989 for the SCs and STs).

Conclusions and suggestions

The employment situation of the SCs and STs in the government sector has received wide publicity, but prejudices and biases continue. This is evident from the Office Memorandum No. 36026/3/85-Estt. (SCT) dated 24 June 1985 which states:

1. The main objective for providing reservation for SCs and STs in appointment to civil posts and services of the Government is not just to give jobs to some persons belonging to these communities and thereby increase their representation in services, but to uplift these people socially and merge them in the mainstream of the nation.

2. It has, however, been pointed out to this department that the SCs and STs officers, after appointment are subjected to harassment and discrimination on grounds of their social origin. It has been pointed out that SC and ST officers are sometimes transferred to far-off places and also placed at insignificant positions. It has also been stated that these officers are not accepted at their places of postings by the concerned superior officers in some cases.

3. In this connection, it is emphasized that the Government should desist from any act of discrimination against members of SC and ST communities on grounds of their social origin.

Members of the SCs and STs are to be found mostly in the unorganized, informal sector and are thus largely unprotected. Because of the non-implementation of the Minimum Wages Act, Equal Remuneration Act, Abolition of Contract Labour Act and Abolition of Bonded Labour Act, etc., in the informal sector, they suffer discrimination and deprivation. A substantial majority of these people are dependent on agriculture, but do not have rights over the land; this leads to situations of meagre wages and bonded labour. The primary sources other than agriculture in the traditional economy are forests, pastures, wasteland and water on which the ordinary people among these communities depend for their living. But the development processes have led to the large-scale displacement of these people from their traditional sources without provision of sufficient rehabilitation activities by the state sector.

The land reforms which were initiated through legislation have not been implemented. This has hindered their employment opportunities. For land reform policy to be more helpful for deprived persons, especially the SCs and STs, there is need for government-led positive measures such as: regular campaigns to detect concealed tenancies by the recording of tenants as occupants; landholdings to be consolidated; more vigorous compilation and updating of land records; adequate financial assistance to develop the allotted land; and restoration of alienated tribal lands through better implementation of existing legislative and executive measures, and the adoption of such legislation by states which do not even have it. Once secure in their land tenure, equitable employment and occupation opportunities for these disadvantaged minorities have a greater chance of success.

Particular affirmative action measures for employment are also linked to better general conditions for these groups. For example, there should be adequate infrastructure plans in the Integrated Rural Development Programme for all areas having a sizeable concentration of SCs and STs so that these people can be gainfully employed. Employment guarantee schemes need to be introduced in the rural areas to help them. The process of changing dry latrines into flush latrines remains to be completed. The members of SCs are employed mainly in this work. These sweepers and scavengers must be categorized as regular employees and they should enjoy the regular service conditions of other employees of the local bodies and state governments. Similarly all the schemes and programmes introduced by the leather corporations have hardly had any impact on the SC families engaged traditionally in leather goods manufacture. This sector needs concrete study and then, on the basis of that, the Department of Industrial Development, the Khadi (homespun cloth) and Village Industries Commission and the representatives of the state governments could plan positive measures to help these deprived people. The dispersed tribals are neglected in the existing development schemes, as many of them do not even find a place in the list of STs. There has been agitation to have such groups included in the lists, and this question is not yet finalized. The functioning of the Tribal Cooperative Development Corporation should be standardized in the different states, a situation which is lacking at present.

As for the government job reservation schemes in place for so long, the representatives of minorities should be included in the selection and recruitment boards for government and semi-government sectors.

Lastly, social awareness campaigns are a must for effective implementation of the various pieces of legislation and any affirmative measures in the employment domain. Illiteracy and ignorance makes these people more vulnerable to discrimination. Thus illiteracy and poverty eradication and the breaking of all kinds of myths and superstitions against them must be a priority.

LEBANON
Dr. Nawaf Kabbara*

3

Studies of the employment practices and programmes of ethnic minorities in Lebanon do not follow the same principles and methods of measurement and assessment as may be found in other countries. Lebanon is divided not only along ethnic lines but, rather, on a religious basis. Whereas the number of ethnic minorities is very limited, the country has 17 officially recognized religious sects, none of whom constitute a majority of the population. These religious demographics have historically necessitated the institution of a delicate power distribution arrangement among the various sects. In this regard, the civil disorder that Lebanon experienced from 1975 until the end of 1991 was, to a certain extent, due to the wishes of certain sects who perceived themselves to be disadvantaged by a proposed change to alter the formula by which the division of power in the country operated.

As a result of the civil strife, an agreement was reached in 1989 by which a new formula for the distribution of power along sectarian lines was agreed upon among the then various religious and political leaders.** Government policies, including employment policies, must be drawn up in accordance with this agreement, which will remain in effect until religious sectarianism is, hopefully, no longer a part of the system.[1]

Flowing from this accord, a rigid quota system was established in the public sector by which employment would be allocated along sectarian lines. Thus, Lebanon's ethnic minorities are dealt with by the positive measures in employment on the basis of their religious denomination and not their status of being part of an ethnic group.

On the other hand, the situation facing persons with disabilities in Lebanon is totally different. Until recently, disabled people in Lebanon were largely outside the concern of the system. Persons with disabilities, like their counterparts in most other countries, experienced the same problems of discrimination and marginalization. Employment policies in both the public and private sectors did not have any provisions to integrate persons with disabilities into mainstream economic activities; instead, these policies exhibited a general attitude of neglect and exclusion. However, beginning in

* Professor, Al-Balamard University, Beirut.

** This agreement is known as the "Taef Agreement" in reference to the Saudi summer resort where the reconciliation conference was held.

1992, this situation began to witness major changes at the governmental level. Disability as a cause has started to become a societal concern. This development stems from a growing level of awareness towards the rights of disabled people, the concern of available rehabilitation and vocational training centres in meeting labour force needs and the portrayal of disabled persons as being a productive part of the labour force. Finally, this change in approach also reflects the increased sophistication of organizations for the disabled both as an effective lobbying force in society and as an agent for empowerment.

This case-study is divided into two sections. The first deals with the question of the employment of ethnic minorities. It focuses on the success of the affirmative action measures dealing with the employment needs of ethnic minorities through their inclusion in the sectarian division of power. The second provides an assessment of the employment situation of disabled persons and the latest changes in government policies and societal positions towards them.

I. EMPLOYMENT OF ETHNIC MINORITIES: THE SECTARIAN SYSTEM AND EMPLOYMENT POLICIES

Lebanon is one of the few countries where employment policies follow a rigid system of balance among the different religious sects that constitute the population.[2] While Lebanon is divided into two main religious groups, Muslims and Christians, 17 religious sects are officially recognized. Most of these sects have their own, separate social and political institutions as well as their own representatives in the Lebanese Chamber of Deputies. On the other hand, there are only a limited number of recognized ethnic groups in Lebanon, mainly Armenians, Kurds and Palestinians, and very small communities of Assyrians and Caledonians.[3] Of these three principal ethnic groups, only Armenians acquired Lebanese nationality and had political access to the system. Nationality was accorded to Kurds and the other above-mentioned groups just recently,* whereas Palestinians are treated as refugees who will eventually be returned to their country once a solution is found to their national situation. Accordingly, Palestinians are denied the right to work in the public sector; however, they are granted permits to work in private enterprise. According to Lebanese law, they cannot be registered in the social security system and employment rights do not apply to them.

In Lebanon, employment policies and practices in both the public and private sectors have been elaborated largely in response to the confessional character of the country. Given the sectarian nature of the Lebanese political system, the religious balance in recruitment in the public sector is closely adhered to. An equal employment policy formula for the two major religious groups (Muslim and Christian) has been in force since the early 1960s. According to this formula, Muslims and Christians should be equally

---

* A presidential decree providing Lebanese nationality to Kurds and other people was announced in July 1994.

employed. However, some public sector positions were reserved for certain sects during the period preceding the adoption of the new Constitution in 1990. In addition, quota divisions did not respect the need for an employment balance among the different sects within the same religious groups. Thus, Maronites had more privileges in the system than other sects such as the Orthodox within the Christian community; the Sunnites were similarly accorded greater privileges within the Muslim population. These privileges were eliminated altogether after the new Constitution was put into place and a new formula for the division of power was adopted.

Pursuant to changes to the Constitution implemented in 1990, employment on the basis of religion in the public service is to be eliminated with the exception of high-level positions which will continue to be divided on sectarian grounds until the system is abolished completely.[4] However, policy changes aside, recruitment for jobs at all echelons of the public administration system continues to respect the old formula of equal appointments for both Christians and Muslims, but without having any one particular position reserved for any given sect.

While these practices amount to a preferential system in public sector employment based on religion, the employment rights of ethnic minorities are included within the quota of each sectarian group. Thus, the quota for Armenians is included within the quota for all Christians and the quota for Kurds is found within the Muslim intake, after they have acquired Lebanese nationality.

If balanced employment is the cornerstone of the sectarian political system, employment practices in the private sector do not follow the same rules. Notwithstanding market forces that respond to competition and efficiency, sectarian employment is largely found in this sector. Accordingly, most businesses that are owned by members of a homogeneous religious group tend to employ people from their own sect and religion.[5] One of the main reasons for this may be geographical; most regions of Lebanon are homogeneous from a sectarian perspective. Another reason may be the strong sectarian solidarity that the social system engenders.

II. EMPLOYMENT OF PERSONS WITH DISABILITIES

The employment of disabled persons does not follow the same principles of quota and balance. If ethnic minorities have limited privileges in employment because of the sectarian system of government, persons with disabilities are to a large extent outside the system, and can be rightly considered as one of the most disadvantaged groups in society. Whereas statistics are available as to the sectarian and ethnic divisions in Lebanese society, there is an almost complete lack of serious studies on the number and categories of disabled persons in the country. It was only in 1981 and as a result of the United Nations Declaration of the International Year for the Disabled that two studies were conducted. The first one was carried out by the Department of Social Affairs in the Ministry of Labour. Disabled people were asked to register in special government offices in different regions of the country. The total number of registered persons was around 40,000.[6] Another study was conducted by a Lebanese NGO, Caritas, according to which the total number of disabled people was estimated to be around 106,000 persons.[7] The Government's report on its application of the United Nations International Covenant on Economic, Social and Cultural Rights estimates that "tens of thousands of people ... have become physically handicapped as a result of the armed conflicts".[8]

Regardless of the real number, Lebanon passed through a period of violence and civil war from 1982 to the end of 1991 and there has been continuing strife in southern Lebanon as a result of the ongoing confrontation between Lebanon and Israel. Many people have been disabled as a result of these events. Accordingly, if 3 per cent of the Lebanese population of 3 million persons is disabled, then the total number of disabled persons is 90,000, close to the Caritas estimate.[9] However, United Nations estimates put the percentage of disabled population at around 10 per cent; using this statistic, there would be approximately 300,000 disabled persons in Lebanon.

If the number of disabled persons is compared with some Lebanese sectarian groups whose total population is under 3 per cent, or between 3 per cent and 10 per cent of the total population, then it becomes clear that disabled people, as a social group, have a similar population in terms of other sectarian and ethnic communities (Catholics, Druze, Armenians, etc.) but do not benefit from the same rights and privileges that these groups are endowed with by the social system. Thus, whereas Armenians have a defined number of representatives in parliament and government, and similar rights in the public sector, disabled persons have not been recognized as a social group with rights and needs that should be met. A similar situation is found in the private sector where social policy has not recognized the need to employ persons with disabilities, thus leaving them outside the mainstream of economic activity. This situation persists despite the fact that, over the last seven years, Lebanon has been host to a series of conferences and seminars concerning the vocational training of persons with disabilities, meetings that have involved the participation of national bodies such as the Lebanese Chamber of Commerce. Individual initiatives may be found, but there has been no serious action to integrate persons with disabilities into the workforce. Many negative stereotypical assumptions still affect employers' attitudes towards persons with disabilities, a situation that has only been aggravated by the recent recession.

An affirmative action policy aimed at integrating disabled persons into the mainstream of economic life does not yet exist. Unlike employment policies in favour of ethnic minorities, which are based on purely political decisions, the mainstream employment of persons with disabilities is usually based on the presence of adequate medical, vocational, social and educational support measures. It also requires the elimination of all architectural and social barriers faced by persons with disabilities.

In order to develop an effective strategy — including affirmative action — for the employment of persons with disabilities, the following issues must be addressed:

— the structural development of rehabilitation services;

— the need for increased medical care, education and vocational training for persons with disabilities;

— the need to develop increased awareness and acceptance in society about the rights of persons with disabilities to be fully integrated into the mainstream of national life;

— the need to increase the strength of the disability movement as a lobby group;

— the need to understand how changes in labour market conditions have an impact on the employment of disabled persons;

— the need for government to pass and implement seriously legislation on behalf of persons with disabilities.

These initiatives must be dealt with simultaneously in order to ensure the successful integration of persons with disabilities into the mainstream economic life of the country. What is the Lebanese situation with reference to each of the above items?

The structures of rehabilitation and related services

The quality and structure of rehabilitation services correlate directly with the provision of employment for disabled people. If integration is the ultimate objective of any disabled person, adequate rehabilitation services are the key to achieving this goal. A disabled person must develop enough knowledge of his or her problems and needs, as well as to be made aware of the different methods available to deal with them.

Rehabilitation services in Lebanon have witnessed major growth in the 1970s and 1980s in terms of quantity and quality. The war was the major impetus for this. Before the events of 1975-91, the number of institutions that dealt with disabled persons was very limited; the total number did not exceed ten associations. Most were concentrated around Beirut.[10] Two major developments took place after law and order broke down in 1975. First, the warring factions felt the need to have their own rehabilitation services to care for their own wounded and disabled combatants. Accordingly, militia and related social groups began investing in the creation of such centres in zones under their control. The second factor was the increasing activities of international funding agencies in Lebanon during the war. The increased number of persons disabled as a result of the war created an urgent social need to open centres and institutions to deal with this tragedy. Social groups, rehabilitation professionals and disabled people grasped the opportunity presented by the presence of international funding agencies to open new centres across the country. These international funding agencies not only provided funds, but also introduced new rehabilitation ideas and trends concerning disability policy. The most important aspect of this intervention was the shift in focus from the need to create large institutions to house and care for disabled people towards the formation of independent living centres and community-based rehabilitation services (CBRS). Thus, the need for institutionalized rehabilitation was limited to mostly a medical and functional need; such services were replaced by rehabilitation programmes within the community itself.[11] This meant that new services were created in the community to give disabled persons a better capacity to overcome societal and structural barriers. Some of these services include transportation, home care, community voluntary services, education and vocational training. This trend resulted in the advancement of the debate concerning the integration of disabled persons. Even though most of these changes related to physically disabled persons, the effect was also felt by all categories of disabled individuals, including, to a large extent, the provision of integrated services for mentally retarded persons. Another outcome was the development by different national NGOs of programmes directed to prepare and facilitate the integration of disabled persons into national economic life. It has also led to the formation by disabled people and rehabilitation professionals of pressure groups that lobby government for the adoption of new legislation and regulations on behalf of disabled persons.

In order to prepare disabled people for work, many associations developed vocational training programmes in different fields including computer sciences and electronics for the physically handicapped, telephone operators and translating for persons with visual impairments, and food packaging for persons with mental impairments. In addition, some NGOs organized funds directed towards assisting disabled persons to develop their own businesses. Moreover, many mainstream vocational training schools have begun admitting disabled students.

Unfortunately, most of the above services were established in Beirut and Mount Lebanon. Disabled people living in rural areas and far from the capital benefit little from them. In addition, the number of people gaining access to the spaces in these programmes is limited due to the shortage of funds available to the Lebanese NGOs and the lack of serious government policy commitments.

A second major barrier to integration faced by persons with disabilities is the unavailability of affordable equipment such as wheelchairs, walkers and urine bags. The Ministry of Health only pays for 80 per cent of the cost of prosthesis and orthosis. And, while the Ministry pays for most of the hospitalization costs of disabled people, drugs and outpatient care are not covered. As a result, disabled people must rely on friends and family or the availability of NGO services; the latter in turn must also rely on international donations to meet the increasing demand.

A third obstacle to the integration of disabled persons in the economic life of the nation is the total absence of accessible and adapted public transportation services. Unlike other countries, Lebanon's public transportation system is almost non-existent. The few buses that do operate in Beirut are not accessible to physically disabled persons. As a result, disabled persons must rely on their own vehicles, or other private means of transport. These are expensive and not always readily available to persons with disabilities. Many disabled persons are denied access to employment on this basis. In a similar vein, another major obstacle to their integration is the lack of accessible worksites. Lebanese law does not enforce accessibility measures on buildings and public spaces. As a result, most construction plans for the reconstruction of the country do not take account of the needs of disabled persons.

Although the above-listed factors militate against the integration of disabled persons, there have been positive developments within the last decade, most notably the formation of pioneer organizations that promote the cause of persons with disabilities and who work to eliminate the discrimination they face. These groups, which include organizations of disabled persons and leaders of different NGOs, have succeeded, through continual persuasion and lobbying, in effecting major changes in government policies and societal attitudes towards disabled people. These changes are discussed below.

An historical overview of Government's concern with disability

The only law that dealt with the question of disability in Lebanon dates from 1973.[12] According to this statute, government is to assume responsibility for the medical, vocational and social needs of disabled people. To achieve this, the legislation created a "National Council for the Welfare of Disabled People" whose mandate was the vocational training and employment of disabled persons in both the public and private sectors and whose composition included representatives of the Ministries of Labour and Social Affairs, Health, Education and Planning. However, the Council only met rarely during the period 1973-75, and ceased functioning entirely after the outbreak of the war in 1975.

In 1978, the Government created a department within the Ministry of Labour and Social Affairs that was responsible for the welfare of disabled persons; its mandate included issues of vocational training and employment.[13] However, following a reorganization of the bureaucracy in 1983, social affairs, including disability issues, became the responsibility of the Ministry of Health. Despite these changes, the level of activity remained at a minimum, due to the ongoing civil strife. This situation changed after 1992.

In 1992, a new government was formed in Lebanon which included, for the first time, a Minister responsible for social and disability affairs. In addition, on 2 December 1992, Lebanon decided to adhere to the United Nations World Programme of Action on behalf of disabled persons. In July 1993, the Parliament created a permanent Ministry of Social Affairs and introduced changes to the 1973 Act concerning disabled persons. The amendments indicated that the integration of disabled persons is a national priority and that all discrimination against them must be eliminated. They also called for positive measures for the provision of employment of disabled persons in both the public and private sectors.

To encourage its implementation, the 1993 legislation changed the composition of the National Council of Disabled People so as to include equal numbers of representatives from the Ministry of Social Affairs, disabled persons themselves, and representatives of NGOs working in the disability field. A sign of its vigorous approach to its mandate is the fact that it meets twice monthly and immediately adopted a programme of action for 1994-95.[14] As part of this programme, the National Council issued a "disability card" as of early 1995, with a view to identifying the category of disability of the person; providing the National Council with comprehensive statistics concerning the number and distribution of disabled persons in Lebanon; and assisting disabled persons in obtaining facilities and concessions in areas such as public transport, medical care, leisure activities and resorts.

In addition, a legal committee was formed in order to present draft legislation to Parliament at the October 1994 session. Its legislative proposals call for the integration of disabled persons in all aspects of national life. They would also require the Government to furnish medical care, education, vocational training and employment for persons with disabilities.[15] Most importantly, they include the introduction of a quota employment system. It should be noted that in April 1993, Lebanon signed a joint communiqué of Arab labour ministers, which sets out proposals for the mandatory employment of disabled persons in both the public and private sectors through the adoption of a 4 per cent quota.[16] The National Council, however, is considering limiting the quota to 2 per cent for companies with 50 or more employees. It is also considering the establishment of a fund, to be financed by organizations that do not respect the quota. Money so generated would be earmarked for vocational training purposes or to assist disabled persons in opening their own businesses.

The National Council has also arranged for an employment pilot project with the National Electric Company of Lebanon to be run from October 1994. The company will employ 60 disabled persons as computer operators. With the help of NGOs, a training programme was organized. In addition, alterations were made to the company buildings so as to make the offices, parking facilities and lavatories accessible.

Unfortunately, not all ministries are responding with equal urgency concerning the development of their own programmes in favour of persons with disabilities. Disability is not yet integrated into the agendas of the Ministries of Education, Vocational Training, Labour, Housing and Transportation, to name but a few. However, this situation may change if the legislation proposed by the National Council is passed by Parliament. Moreover, the National Council, in cooperation with organized pressure groups, is to develop an effective lobbying strategy towards government and ministerial departments to ensure serious consideration of disabled peoples' rights. A dialogue should be opened with representatives of the private sector, in order to convince them to promote the employment of persons with disabilities within their enterprises. Most disabled people should be integrated into the mainstream; sheltered workshops should only be used for people with multiple disabilities or who are severely mentally impaired. Finally, new technology presents disabled people with a marvellous opportunity for employment. Developments in electronics and computer sciences have diminished the importance of physical work given to disabled people when competing in these fields with able-bodied individuals. All these factors are vital to open the way for a normal, productive life for persons with disabilities.

Notes

[1] The Lebanese Constitution, 23 May 1926, amended 1943 and revised 1990, article 5.

[2] For recent data on the population's confessional breakdown see McDowell, 1996.

[3] Berg, 1980, p. 82.

[4] The Lebanese Constitution, article 95.

[5] Dubar and Nasr, 1976, pp. 309-310.

[6] Husseini and Houri, 1982.

[7] Caritas, 1993.

[8] Initial report under articles 16 and 17 of the Covenant: United Nations, 1993a, para. 41.

[9] From research studies conducted by the Council for Development and Reconstruction in Lebanon.

[10] Kinan, 1993.

[11] From 1988 until 1994, 16 CBRS programmes were opened in different areas of the country.

[12] Act No. 11/73 of 31 Jan. 1973.

[13] Decree No. 421 of 23 June 1977.

[14] The programme is published in *Asda Al-Mouakeen,* Jan. 1994.

[15] *Asda Al-Mouakeen,* July 1994.

[16] The full communiqué of the joint Arab report concerning disabled persons is found in *Asda Al-Mouakeen,* Apr. 1994.

MALAYSIA

4

I. CHARACTERIZATION OF ETHNIC GROUPS AND PERSONS WITH DISABILITIES

Composition of Malaysia's population

Malaysia is a multiracial and multi-religious country of 17.5 million persons; 59 per cent are ethnic Malays, 32.1 per cent are Chinese, 8.2 per cent Indians and 0.7 per cent others. The country is rapidly urbanizing; 51 per cent of the population resides in urban areas as compared to 34 per cent in 1980 (1991 Census).

Broadly speaking, Malaysia's ethnic groups fall into two main categories. Those whose cultural affinities are indigenous to the region and to one another, are known as Bumiputra, or "sons of the soil". The dominant Bumiputra are ethnic Malays. In addition, there are non-Bumiputra groups whose cultural affinities may be traced from outside the indigenous region.[1] While there are other ways in which the population of Malaysia may be categorized, such as Muslim/non-Muslim, or Malay/non-Malay, for the purposes of this analysis, this study adopts a Bumiputra/non-Bumiputra categorization. To illustrate this categorization, a marginalized minority within the Bumiputra category are the ethnic Orang Asli (original people — aborigines), who comprise 0.5 per cent of the population (approximately 72,000 persons).[2]

Disabled persons are one of the disadvantaged communities in Malaysian society, comprising about 180,000 persons. This figure is based on a level of disability of 1 per cent adopted by the Malaysian Government.[3] Compared to other countries, this seems a rather low and arbitrary estimate. On the other hand, according to the Department of Social Welfare there are 50,116 persons registered as disabled. It should be noted in this respect, however, that registration as a disabled person is on a voluntary basis. It is also important to note that there is no statistical breakdown available on the ethnic or racial composition of the disabled community.

As Malaysia's economic growth is 8.5 per cent there are numerous employment opportunities for all communities. Total employment is expected to rise from 6.6 million in 1990 to 9 million by the year 2000.

Because employment is growing at an annual rate of 2.9 per cent, the unemployment rate is expected to fall from 6 per cent in 1990 to 4 per cent by the end of the 1990s.[4] In this regard, the National Labour Policy envisions a full employment strategy. Furthermore, the policy states that "employment should reflect the racial composition of the country in all occupations and at all levels of management".[5]

Currently, there is a shortage of labour, which has resulted in an increased presence of migrant workers, especially from Indonesia, the Philippines and Bangladesh. These persons are mostly employed in the construction industry as well as domestic and manual labour. However, although there are ample employment opportunities for all, segments of the Malaysian population indicate they experience discrimination on account of their ethnic origins or disability or both.

There are only two laws directly dealing with employment: the Employment Act of 1955 and the Industrial Relations Act of 1955, both revised in 1981. The 1957 Constitution, in article 153, recognizes the Malays and the indigenous peoples of Sarawak and Sabah as Bumiputras with protected rights and privileges. Its article 8(5) states that the general principle of equality does not invalidate or prohibit, among others, any provision for the protection or advancement of the aboriginal peoples of the Malay Peninsula (including the reservation of land) or the reservation to aborigines of a reasonable proportion of suitable positions in the public service. Thus, the majority population, rather than an ethnic minority, is singled out for special attention. This constitutional affirmative action, based on the disparities in living conditions follows pro-Malay preference first instituted by the colonial administration. It has been the subject of comment by both academics and politicians: as it is not a temporary measure, does it amount to discrimination by perpetuating a division of labour between the ethnic groups? Is it rather a special measure for a group requiring extra assistance, in the sense of Article 5(2) of the Discrimination (Employment and Occupation) Convention, 1958 (No. 111)?[6] Replying to a query from the Government on the comparability of the provision within the Convention, it was pointed out that the State's decision to adopt special measures to ensure protection and assistance for specific categories of persons "would have to be made in good faith and would have to be reasonable, having regard to conditions actually obtaining in the country".[7]

II. ETHNICITY AND EMPLOYMENT OPPORTUNITIES

It must be noted that there is very little research or literature available with reference to discrimination experienced by Malaysian minorities on account of race and/or ethnic origin.[8] There is, however, some literature concerning discrimination in the context of the general poverty issue relating to the Indian minorities,[9] communal politics and land rights of the indigenous peoples of the Peninsula, the Orang Asli.[10] Recent literature tends to focus on the market potential in the context of industrialization and labour markets;[11] even the two standard texts on industrial relations make no reference to the issue of racial discrimination.[12] The focus of trade unions has been on general workers' rights and working conditions (such as wages) and not on racial or ethnic discrimination.[13]

An appreciation of the current situation in Malaysia, especially the reports of discrimination being experienced by non-Bumiputras (i.e. Indians and Chinese) in the public service, may only be understood in light of the race riots of 13 May 1969 and the policies that ensued from them. Prior to the 1969 riots, there existed socio-economic imbalances along racial lines in that the ethnic Malay community was economically disadvantaged. Furthermore, the perpetuation of this situation was seen to be not conducive for national stability and unity.[14] As the Prime Minister indicated, "in view of the historic economic deprivation of the Malay community, some positive discrimination and affirmative action is inevitable, especially since nominal Malay political hegemony has been assured since the late colonial period".[15]

In an effort to redress this imbalance, the Government in 1970 introduced the New Economic Policy (NEP). This was "socio-economic engineering designed to bring about a more equitable distribution of wealth between the different races or groups in the various strata of society".[16] The NEP has two policy objectives: eradicating poverty irrespective of race, and restructuring society to reduce the identification of race with economic function. It introduced a quota system in various areas, for example, admission to universities, equity ownership and employment and promotion in the public service so that it would more closely reflect the racial composition of the country. This programme was put in place for a 20-year period.

However, according to one commentator, far from having positive connotations:

For most Malaysians, the NEP has now narrowly come to refer to the Government's efforts to create and consolidate the Malay business and middle classes, especially the goal of increasing the percentage of share capital from 2.5 per cent in 1970 to 30 per cent in 1990. With such an emphasis, the NEP implementation has seen the growth of the public sector, as well as officially sanctioned ethnic discrimination and state intervention, inevitably causing considerable resentment, especially among the non-Malays, and to a lesser extent, among non-Muslim Bumiputras (indigens) as well. Despite such widespread resentment and opposition to the NEP among non-Malays, abandonment of the NEP would be very threatening to a Malay community long nurtured on the NEP and led to believe that all the gains they have made since 1970 have been due to the NEP.[17]

III. IMPACT OF AFFIRMATIVE ACTION PROGRAMMES FOR ETHNIC GROUPS

At the end of the 20-year period, there was much discussion on both the positive as well as the negative aspects of the NEP period as well as what future policies should be adopted. Insights into the programme's impact in the employment sector are given in one study[18] which documented the non-Bumiputra resentment. It found that ethnic quotas favouring Bumiputra applicants to institutions of higher learning have incensed non-Bumiputras, being part of what it refers to as a whole array of "state policies and programmes" and "special privileges" which are geared towards Bumiputra interests in housing, education, commerce, the professions and agriculture. Muzaffar also notes that there is a preference to provide state contracts in construction to Bumiputra-controlled enterprises.[19]

In the public sector, for example, Bumiputras now account for the largest share of employment, with a concomitant decline in non-Bumiputra representation. The Outline Perspective Plan (OPP2) states that "the restructuring of employment will also take into account the need for higher participation of non-Bumiputra in sectors in which they are now under-represented. Accordingly, a better representation of non-Bumiputras in public sector appointments, such as at the middle and senior levels of the civil service, will improve the ethnic structure of employment".[20] Similarly, leaders of the Malaysian Chinese community have called for a more balanced racial representation, noting that a more equitable balance would lead to increased sensitivity as to the multiracial character of the country. Malaysian Chinese leaders recognize that the quota programme will continue, but that it will be reviewed. Also, they were given assurances that there would be an increase in the number of Chinese civil servants by 20,400 and Indians by 11,200 as compared to 15,200 for Bumiputras.

While there is no documented evidence of discrimination as a result of affirmative action measures, such as through court cases or as a result of industrial action, many non-Bumiputras informally have alleged being victims of discrimination in employment (recruitment, promotions and recruitment to senior positions). In this regard, one notable case received media attention. A 52-year old person sued the Malacca Municipal Council for unconstitutional discrimination, alleging he was denied a promotion. While the formal allegations concerned age discrimination, the issue of race was informally at issue, inasmuch as the individual concerned was of Indian origin.[21]

Malaysian legislation and employment policies formally do not permit discrimination. However, it is not possible to know whether there is *de facto* discrimination at the level of programme implementation. The Government has acknowledged this possibility by recognizing the necessity of correcting the under-representation of non-Bumiputras in the public sector through the National Development Policy outlined in the OPP2 (1991-2000) mentioned above.

As for private sector employment, in the professional and technical categories, Bumiputra representation exceeded the 50 per cent target set in the First Outline Perspective Plan (OPP1), reaching 61.8 per cent by 1990. However, a large proportion of the Bumiputras found in these occupational groups are employed as teachers and nurses. In the administrative and managerial occupational groups, the Bumiputra representation also improved, from 22.4 per cent in 1970 to 31.3 per cent in 1990. But this is below their targeted representation level of 49.3 per cent; the failure to attain the target reflects low Bumiputra representation at the managerial and supervisory levels in the manufacturing and service sectors.[22]

In the post-NEP period, the quota programme will continue in order to correct the still existing imbalances in the professional and private sectors.

For the same reason, and to encourage a larger Bumiputra candidate pool in the professional, managerial and technical categories, the existing affirmative action measures relating to admission to institutions of higher learning will be maintained.[23] In this regard, when tabling the OPP2, the Prime Minister remarked that "the faster we move towards redressing ethnic imbalances, the lesser will be the need to have privileges for the Bumiputra".[24]

While, as indicated above, there are informal allegations of non-Bumiputras experiencing discrimination as a result of affirmative action in the public sector, the situation in private enterprise is characterized by low Bumiputra representation. Certain ethnic groups have high concentration in particular business sectors; if it were not for the intervention of Government, the Bumiputra presence would be minimal. The press has cited several instances where government officials have alleged incidents of private sector companies discriminating against Bumiputras (failure to promote, lay-offs and harassment from superiors). In the citations, the Government indicated that these enterprises were not conducting themselves in accordance with the spirit of the NEP.[25]

Persons of Indian ethnic origin also experience inequitable levels of representation in certain professions. Moreover, in those professions where Indians do experience equitable levels of representation, their increase in absolute terms has been much slower than those of the various Bumiputra communities and the Chinese. As a result, the share of Indian employment in these professions has declined continuously since 1970.[26] Two interrelated reasons have been advanced to account for this situation. First, there have been no increases in the levels of intake of Indian students by colleges and universities, both in qualitative and quantitative dimensions. Second, in the poor State of Tamil, vernacular schools do not adequately prepare students from this ethnic group for post-primary education.[27]

The OPP2 recognizes that while all communities have progressed since 1970, the socio-economic position of certain groups within the Bumiputra community such as the Orang Asli and the indigenous groups in Sabah and Sarawak, as well as Indians within the non-Bumiputra Indians, have lagged behind the achievements of others. In the implementation of the NEP, the needs of these groups will be given particular attention to enable them to benefit equitably from the growth in the economy and the implementation of developmental programmes.[28]

IV. AFFIRMATIVE ACTION MEASURES FOR EMPLOYMENT OF PERSONS WITH DISABILITIES

Government policies

There are scarcely any research publications in Malaysia with reference to disability in general or concerning employment discrimination experienced by persons with disabilities, in particular.[29]

Among government policies concerning employment opportunities for these persons appear the National Labour Policy, the quota scheme, the tax policy, grants and support measures and general statutory measures.

The Government's National Labour Policy makes two references to persons with disabilities:

— that employment policy objectives will continue to stress the need for increasing the participation of persons with disabilities in the workforce; and

— that it is an employment policy objective to generate employment opportunities for persons with disabilities.[30]

In 1989, the Government introduced an employment quota policy whereby 1 per cent of positions in the public sector would be reserved for persons with disabilities; in 1990, this policy was extended to the private sector.

In addition to the quota scheme, three tax incentives are provided to private sector enterprises in order to encourage the provision of job opportunities for disabled people: enterprises may deduct expenditures in respect of the furnishing of any equipment needed to accommodate a disabled employee; enterprises are permitted a double tax deduction with respect to the remuneration paid to each employee who is mentally or physically disabled; and enterprises are allowed a double tax deduction concerning expenses incurred in the training of disabled persons.

However, while the tax rules provide for a double deduction for remuneration paid to persons with disabilities, eligibility to claim this deduction is subject to the employer proving that the employee is physically and mentally disabled and is not able to perform the work of a normal person. Because of the vagueness of this definition, it has been recognized that many employers find that they are unable to claim the deduction. There is an indication that the Government is prepared to reconsider the way in which disability is defined for this purpose: the comment was made that "the definition of the handicapped person should be based on physical disability and not on work performance".[31]

The Government has made available three types of employment related grants and/or supports for persons with disabilities:[32] a business grant of 2,000 ringgits is available to disabled persons beginning a business (in 1992, 109 disabled individuals received this grant); under a work incentive allowance, 50 ringgits are given to employed disabled persons earning between 20-30 ringgits to increase income and to act as an encouragement to remain employed; and a fund exists to purchase equipment such as wheelchairs or hearing-aids for disabled persons (in 1992, 327 individuals received equipment using this fund valued at 239,810 ringgits). A further support measure has been the creation, by the Government, of a National Committee for the Promotion of Employment Opportunities for persons with disabilities in the private sector with the Minister of Human Resources as its chairperson. One of the first activities of this Committee was the launching of an awareness campaign to encourage the employment of disabled persons.

As for statutory measures, there is no direct legislation ensuring the rights of disabled persons in Malaysian society. Constitutionally, however, a disabled person may claim rights pursuant to article 8 of the Federal Constitution. Clause 1 of this article states that "all persons are equal before the law and entitled to the protection of the law"; clause 2 qualifies this by stating that "there shall be no discrimination against citizens on the grounds only of religion, race, descent or place of birth". However, disability is not an unconstitutional ground of discrimination specified in article 8.[33]

The dominant view held by the majority of Malaysians is that charity is the best assistance that can be provided to "helpless" disabled persons. In this regard, there is an urgent need to develop alternative public perceptions based on the notion that disabled persons have the same constitutional citizenship rights and responsibilities, including the right of full participation, as other members of Malaysian society.

Access to public facilities

In 1990, the Uniform Building By-Laws of 1984 were amended to provide that all new public buildings will be required to provide facilities for persons with disabilities. Under the amendments, owners of existing buildings have three years to complete the adaptations.

In 1992, the Malaysian Standard Code of Practice for access by disabled persons to public buildings was released by the Standards and Industrial Research Institute of Malaysia (SIRIM). This standard specifies the basic requirements for the accessibility to public buildings and facilities by disabled persons. It applies to all buildings that persons with disabilities might use, both in the course of their employment and as members of the general public as visitors. If both these instruments are gazetted by all the state authorities, it will then be obligatory for developers to take into consideration the needs of disabled persons when planning the construction of public facilities. This would have an important impact on the socio-economic integration of persons with disabilities.

V. IMPACT OF AFFIRMATIVE ACTION PROGRAMMES FOR THE DISABLED

The above-outlined policies and programmes introduced by the Government have proven to be very positive steps. By the end of 1991, there were 744 disabled persons employed in the public sector. Following appeals by the Human Resources Minister, a total of 2,152 positions were offered by private sector firms between 1990 and 1991. However, of this number, only 1,249 jobs were filled by persons with disabilities. Ganapathy has identified five reasons for this:

— there is no central registry of disabled persons seeking employment, partly the fault of a lack of coordination on the part of both government and voluntary agencies;

— there is prejudice against the employment of persons with disabilities;

— many public facilities are not physically accessible to disabled persons;

— employers are reluctant to modify or adapt machinery or facilities to accommodate persons with disabilities; and

— the majority of positions offered (70 per cent) were located in the Klang Valley.[34]

It is also noted that many existing voluntary organizations that serve persons with disabilities have not furnished adequate preparation to their clients. As a result, these organizations were ill-prepared to respond to the Government's call to provide employment in the expanding employment market. This inability on the part of the NGO sector demonstrates that much more work must be done to prepare persons with disabilities for the world of work. Existing vocational training must be able to provide disabled persons with the requisite skills to function efficiently and effectively in an integrated work setting. At the same time, new avenues for the vocational training of persons with disabilities must be explored as well as renewing and upgrading existing programmes.

Another measurement of the impact of affirmative action measures can be drawn from the existence of formal complaints of discrimination and data on how such complaints are handled.

The Industrial Relations Department (IRD) does not keep records of complaints of discrimination based on disability. Moreover, if such complaints were received from persons with disabilities, they would, by necessity, be based on other grounds, such as wrongful dismissal, wage disputes, etc. That said, this study came across two cases of discrimination experienced by disabled individuals, both of whom are wheelchair users.

In the first case, a disabled person was dismissed by a volunteer organization. As it was alleged the dismissal was without valid cause, she filed a complaint with the IRD. Negotiations ensued, and the woman was reinstated. In another case that received media attention, a disabled person was released when he could not perform certain duties that were located on an inaccessible floor of the building where he worked. Following a complaint to the IRD in which he claimed he was dismissed on account of his disability, the person concerned received higher compensation for loss of earnings.

Apart from these two specific cases, there have been narrative accounts of discrimination reported in the media. For example, the President of the Society of Hearing-Impaired has said deaf persons have little scope for employment despite being qualified. He cited the case of a deaf university graduate who had applied for a senior-level position in the civil service, but was faced with problems when medical officers were afraid to approve his medical fitness for work because he was deaf.[35] In another case, a deaf electrician reported that he was being discriminated against (denied the chance to do the more complex electrical tasks) because of his disability. A paraplegic woman reported that "getting a job is already considered a success due to society's prejudice towards the disabled in the workplace ... This sort of discrimination among employers and colleagues aren't *(sic)* displayed openly but I could sense it when I first started working. It took a long time for me to feel accepted and not being made to feel differently from the rest".[36]

VI. CONCLUSIONS CONCERNING PERSONS WITH DISABILITIES

The need for different approaches in the rehabilitation and employment of disabled persons is clear. Disabled persons must no longer be viewed as charity objects deserving patronizing care. Disabled persons must be seen to be what they are; human beings with human potential and capacity for integration in society. Disabled persons have the basic right to share in the economic growth of Malaysia. They are not asking for hand-outs but, rather, for equal opportunities to live as responsible citizens of the country. In this regard, a change in perspective is increasingly in evidence. While the dominant approach in Malaysia remains one which reaffirms a "charity" model, there are clear signs that affirmative action programmes and other initiatives of government and NGOs which seek to empower persons with disabilities are resulting in increased employment opportunities.

Notes

[1] Malaysia Department of Statistics, 1995, pp. 32-35 and 38-40.

[2] Centre for Community Studies, 1994.

[3] Jaysooria et al., 1992, pp. 232-265.

[4] Malaysia, 1991, p. 163.

[5] idem., 1992, p. 8.

[6] ILO, 1988, para. 147; Arles, 1971.

[7] ILO memorandum sent to the Minister of External Affairs of the Federation of Malaysia, *Official Bulletin,* 1959, p. 397.

[8] Koyakoti, 1981, p. 13.

[9] Ramasdamy, 1994; Ramachandran, 1994.

[10] International Work Group for Indigenous Affairs, 1995, pp. 139-141.

[11] Joma, 1993, 1994.

[12] Mills, 1984; Ayadurai, 1992.

[13] Shari, 1980.

[14] Mahathir, 1991, p. 10.

[15] Jomo, 1989, p. 15.

[16] Mahathir, 1991, p. 10.

[17] Jomo, 1989, p. 15.

[18] Muzaffar, 1987, pp. 51-52.

[19] ibid., p. 57.

[20] Malaysia, 1991, p. 115.

[21] *The Star*, 3 Apr. 1987.

[22] Malaysia, 1991, p. 47, item 2.42.

[23] ibid., p. 114, item 4.57.

[24] Mahathir, 1991, p. 11.

[25] *New Straits Times,* 27 Mar. 1984; 27-28 Feb. 1987; 23 June 1989; 10 Apr. 1990.

[26] Malaysia, 1991, p. 11, item 1.31.

[27] Malaysian Indian Congress, 1992, p. 15.

[28] Malaysia, 1991, p. 16, item 1.49.

[29] Chew, 1992.

[30] Malaysia, 1992, items 3.2 and 4.1.3.

[31] *Malay Mail,* 24 Nov. 1993.

[32] Ariff, 1993.

[33] Suffian, 1976, p. 216.

[34] Ganapathy, 1992, p. 1.

[35] *Malay Mail,* 8 July 1992.

[36] *The Star,* 17 Feb. 1993.

NORWAY
John Bernhard Henriksen*

5

I. AFFIRMATIVE ACTION PROGRAMMES TO OVERCOME DISCRIMINATION IN EMPLOYMENT AGAINST DISABLED PERSONS

Of a labour force of 68.2 per cent of the total Norwegian population, disabled persons aged between 16 and 66 years account for 11 per cent. In 1990, the number of persons drawing disability benefits amounted to 9.3 per cent of the working-age population. The National Action Programme for the Disabled defines disability as the imbalance between an individual's capacities and the requirements of the surroundings in all fields which are essential for establishment of independence and a social life. Only inabilities of a permanent character are recognized as disability under this definition and this definition is not identical to the legal definition of disability, which also recognizes temporary stages of inability. Since the National Action Programme definition focuses on disability in relation to the surroundings, attention is not only focused on the handicap of the person, as is the case in the legal definition, but also on adjustable factors in the surroundings and working environment, factors which can be the subject of affirmative action measures.

The legislative framework has played an important role in establishing equal employment opportunities through affirmative action. Article 110 of the Constitution states that every person has the right to be employed, and places the onus on the state authorities to promote the conditions so that anyone who possesses the capacity to work can have an income by working. The specific legislation relating to employment, the Norwegian Working Environment Act, No. 4, of 4 February 1977, in section 13 concerning working conditions, regulates the employment of disabled workers. The employer has a legal obligation to ensure that physical conditions such as doors, steps, sanitary installations and technical facilities, as far as this is possible and reasonable, are accessible to disabled employees. This requirement covers both applicants for employment and persons already employed. This law also contains regulations under which employers are

---

* Lawyer, Norway.

legally obliged, as far as possible, to make the necessary adjustments to the working environment whenever an employee becomes disabled due to an accident, disease, etc. Moreover, the workers have the right to preferential treatment, and the right to continue in their usual jobs, with the work surroundings being adjusted, if necessary and in so far as is reasonable, so that the workers can continue in their usual job. When it is necessary, because of disability, to transfer the worker to a new job, this cannot be done without consultations with the worker and the shop steward concerned.

Both article 110 of the Constitution and section 13 in the Working Environment Act guarantee equality in employment for disabled persons, both in the public and the private sector. However, an important aspect of the Working Environment Act is that it goes further than giving a passive guarantee: it obliges the employer to make special provision for disabled workers and employees in the working environment in order to accommodate the current disability.

Adherence to international instruments has also facilitated the adoption — and acceptance by the social partners — of affirmative action measures. Norway ratified the ILO Vocational Rehabilitation and Employment (Disabled Persons) Convention, 1983 (No. 159), on 13 August 1984. Norway has thereby committed itself at the international level to ensuring that appropriate vocational rehabilitation measures are made available to all categories of disabled persons. In addition, it has to promote employment opportunities for disabled persons in the open labour market (Article 3 of the Convention). The Convention also states that the State shall formulate, implement and periodically review the national policy on vocational rehabilitation and employment of disabled persons (Article 2).

At the national level, the Government has for a number of years adopted national action programmes for disabled persons. These are periodic action programmes, the present one being currently in force for the period 1994-97.

The history of these action programmes at the national level commenced with a very general form of action programme for the 1980s, which was adopted in 1983. The government ministries involved at that time had been obliged merely to make annual reports and reviews of their implementation of the programme. Yet even in those early days, during the preparatory stage of the action programme, organizations of disabled persons also participated in their formulation. The first formal National Action Programme was for the period 1990-93, when the Government gave its first systematic attention to special measures in order to achieve full participation and equality for disabled persons in society. This first programme contained broad policy aims as well as concrete measures, reflected in the following summary of its objectives with regard to employment: (a) a governmental report *(Stortingsmelding)* had to be tabled on "Vocational rehabilitation and jobs for disabled persons"; (b) there was an increase in resources granted to the State Labour Market Department/Administration earmarked for disabled persons; (c) there was to be an increase in the total number of employment initiatives and jobs for disabled persons; (d) experiments and research were to be carried out in order to test the impact of the new employment initiatives and jobs created for disabled persons; and (e) rational transport services for disabled persons were to be developed.

One concrete implementation of these aims was Parliament's *(Storting)* decision in November 1991 to reorganize the specialized supplementary services for vocational rehabilitation of the disabled within the Labour Market Administration. The reorganization took place in 1992: the four centralized labour market institutes were discontinued in that form, and their services were henceforth provided through Employment Counselling Offices, which were established in all 19 counties. The aim of this reform was to provide services closer to the users, and provide vocational rehabilitation in an integrated setting. The role of the Employment Counselling Offices is to give specialized professional support to the Employment Offices, which have the primary role in vocational rehabilitation. The Employment Counselling Offices assist in assessing and developing rehabilitation plans for the individual. A national centre for vocational rehabilitation was established in Oslo, which has special responsibilities towards particular groups of disabled persons, e.g. persons with sensory impairment, brain damage or severe mobility impairment.

Another result was the April 1992 government report to the *Storting* on vocational rehabilitation and employment for disabled persons, sickness benefits and rehabilitation benefits. Prepared by the Ministry of Labour in collaboration with the Ministry of Social Affairs and Health, its aim was to develop a coherent policy to counteract the trend of excluding workers from the labour market because of their ill health and disability. This trend was evidenced by the sharp increase over the previous decade in the numbers of persons of working age receiving disability pensions or sickness benefits from the National Insurance System. The strategies outlined in the report, which were followed up by appropriate legislation, consisted of a two-pronged approach: on the one hand, the medical criteria for receipt of disability pensions and sickness benefits were defined more restrictively; on the other hand, increased emphasis was given to vocational rehabilitation. Work and active rehabilitation measures were to be the first choice, before the passive receipt of social security benefits. Further social security benefits were in turn to be used more actively in vocational rehabilitation. The strategies included increased emphasis on early intervention, and emphasis on integration in the ordinary labour market. The role of employers was recognized to be crucial. The legislative follow-up (in the form of an amendment to the National Insurance Act in June 1993) ensured that, as from 1 January 1994, the responsibility for organizing and financing all active rehabilitation measures would lie with the Labour Market Administration, in line with the general policy on integration of disabled people. Thus, vocational and employment services for disabled people are now provided within the same framework as for other non-disabled jobseekers.

Data being so vital to positive labour market interventions, in addition to the Labour Market Administration's tasks of job placement, payment of benefits and administration of labour market schemes, in 1991 it created a register of vocationally disabled people within the so-called "TOTAL" system.

One of the central policies to promote employment opportunities for people with disabilities in the labour market is increased emphasis on temporary "work experience" programmes. Since 1991 there has also been an integration subsidies scheme (started as a three-year experiment) aimed at helping to integrate particularly vulnerable groups of the vocationally disabled into ordinary working life. In 1992 the new approach of "supported employment" to integrate groups such as people with mental retardation into ordinary employment was introduced. It offers elements of affirmative action in the form of personal support and follow-up to disabled persons after job placement so as to help them adapt to the work environment. Also in 1992, a scheme of financial support was established for interpretation services to the deaf and persons with hearing problems, in cases where special technology is necessary to enable them to function effectively in suitable employment, or to undergo education or vocational training. In 1993 the Working Life Advisory Service was created within the Labour Market Administration to assist employers in organizing workplace rehabilitation; it is organized at the county level throughout the country.

The National Action Programme for 1994-97 is a direct result of the process which grew out of the first general programme of 1983 and blossomed with the numerous employment-related initiatives in the 1990-93 Action Programme. The current programme is comprised of a broad policy for a broad range of action, and covers all sectors of society. Following the basic philosophy that a society which includes disabled persons is one which benefits everyone, the principal aim of the programme is the achievement of full participation and equality in society — including in employment — for disabled persons. The National Action Programme covers five main groups of disability: (a) movement/mobility impairment; (b) hearing impairment; (c) sight/vision impairment; (d) psychological impairment; and (e) concealed disability (e.g. diabetes, psychological problems, heart problems, dyslexia, allergy).

The employment section of the 1994-97 National Action Programme recognizes that disabled persons face many types of problems in relation to equality in access to employment including: the average level of education is lower amongst disabled persons compared to the rest of the population, in particular for male disabled persons; the level of income is lower for families which include a disabled person; disabled persons more often than others have financial difficulties; disabled persons are under-represented in the labour market; disabled persons generally have shorter working hours than others; and many disabled persons are forced to leave their jobs due to lack of arrangements to accommodate their problems.

Its objectives with regard to employment are:

(a) the use of labour market training courses as a rehabilitation measure (to include ordinary courses as well as special courses for some disability groups; the Ministry of Local Government and Employment (MLGE) is responsible for these courses);

(b) positive job creation to increase the total number of employment initiatives or jobs, the responsible ministry being the MLGE;

(c) increasing the responsibility within the State Labour Market Department/Administration concerned with the labour situation of disabled persons, again with the responsible ministry being the MLGE;

(d) increasing the skill and knowledge within the State Labour Market Department/Administration itself on the subject of rehabilitation, the responsible ministry being the MLGE;

(e) the preparation of a special study concerning rehabilitation at the Oppland District High School *(Oppland Distriktshøyskole)* with the responsible ministry being the Ministry of Educational Affairs; and

(f) the establishment of an advisory service within the State Labour Market Department/Administration in order to help and support the employers with internal rehabilitation of their workers; again the MLGE is the responsible ministry.

Coupled with these objectives is an economic incentive in the form of time-limited wage subsidies to employers to facilitate placement of disabled workers in permanent jobs or "work experience" programmes.[1]

Vital to the overall success of the above-described legislative and policy action to promote the employment of persons with disabilities is the State Council of Disabled Persons (SCDP) *(Rådet for Funksjonshemmede)*. It is the advisory body of the Norwegian Government for all issues concerning disability and also advises other public institutions and bodies on disability issues. Its composition reflects current policy of full integration of these persons in all aspects of society: the Council has 11 members currently including politicians, leaders of associations of disabled and handicapped persons (such as the Norwegian Association for Persons with Heart and Lung Diseases), heads of social and medical affairs departments, as well as of employment departments, and an academic. The SCDP's mandate is to consider questions concerning disabled persons and their situation; to stimulate dialogue on these issues with other public institutions; to express their opinion on questions submitted to it; to gather information about the needs and problems of disabled persons, and to try to find possible solutions; and to collect and disseminate information so as to sensitize the public at large.

Its 1992-95 programme lists the following aims for its work concerning education and employment opportunities for disabled persons: (a) to strengthen public cooperation; (b) to strengthen the skill and knowledge within the rehabilitation system for dealing with this issue; (c) to allocate more resources to the public rehabilitation system; (d) to improve the situation with regard to technological advances to accommodate disabilities in the physical working environment; (e) to provide more and better suited jobs for disabled persons in the public sector as well as in the private sector; and (f) to improve salary and working conditions for disabled persons.

II. THE IMPACT OF AFFIRMATIVE ACTION MEASURES FOR THE DISABLED

In Norway the legal rights related to employment of disabled persons set a good general context for formal and voluntary positive measures to increase their workforce participation. In addition, the affirmative action programmes adopted over the last decade to overcome discrimination and to improve their general working conditions have met with solid societal support.

However, it appears still to be difficult to achieve equality in access to employment for disabled persons, evidenced by the fact that today there is a high percentage of unemployment among disabled persons. According to the National Statistics Bureau, the percentage of disabled persons in employment is approximately 50 per cent compared with the rest of the labour force. This situation is the same for both female and male disabled persons. The current generally high rate of unemployment in the population also has negative consequences for disabled persons. Due to lack of jobs in the labour market, competition is harder and disabled jobseekers are often the hardest hit.

This study of the affirmative action measures taken to date points to two key factors in overcoming the barriers which continue to exist. First, higher education for disabled persons is clearly one of the main elements for an improvement in their situation in the labour market. As mentioned earlier, the average educational level is much lower among disabled persons than among the rest of the labour force. Education is therefore very important in order to ensure that disabled persons obtain equal opportunities for gainful employment in the labour market. Second, preferential treatment in favour of disabled persons in employment, in a setting of society's acceptance of their place in the workforce rather than viewing them as objects of charity, should involve representatives of this population group and should be as varied as possible. For example, by increasing the financial incentives available to employers for more direct hiring and for adapting the physical working environment (including sensitization courses to adapt the mental attitudes of fellow workers) might well have immediate results.

III. AFFIRMATIVE ACTION PROGRAMMES TO OVERCOME DISCRIMINATION IN EMPLOYMENT AGAINST ETHNIC MINORITIES

This study of affirmative action programmes established to achieve equality in employment for disabled persons and ethnic minorities, drawing on analytical studies and evaluations concerning their impact, does not deal with the indigenous people of Norway (the Samis) who are not referred to as "ethnic" minorities, but rather the employment equity of Norwegians of different ethnic origin. The equal opportunities provided to the Samis, both *de jure* and *de facto,* are well documented elsewhere.[2] There are no affirmative action programmes to overcome discrimination in employment against Samis as such situations are no longer an issue. Key Sami bodies such as the Sami Parliament focus on collective, developmental issues.

According to the National Statistics Bureau, the ethnic minorities in Norway in 1993 (of a total immigrant population of 154,012, representing 3.6 per cent of the total population) were comprised mainly of immigrants from Africa, Asia and Latin America (63,198 being 41 per cent of all immigrants).

As mentioned above, the Constitution states that every person has the right to be employed. The more specific labour legislation, the Working Environment Act, No. 4, of 1977, allows employers (by virtue of section 55A) to request, or by other means to obtain during recruitment procedures, information on the political, religious or cultural views of job applicants, including their trade union membership. The rule is that an employer does not have the right to demand such information, but exceptions can be made if the information is required owing to the nature of the situation or if the main sphere of activity of the employer is such as to promote particular political, religious or cultural views and the post is of importance in the achievement of that objective. This provision — in so far as it affects religious discrimination — has been the subject of comment in the context of Norway's ratification of the ILO's Discrimination (Employment and Occupation) Convention, 1958 (No. 111). Under that Convention, Norway has the obligation to declare and pursue a national policy designed to promote, by methods appropriate to national conditions and practice, equality of opportunity and treatment in employment and occupation, with a view to eliminating any discrimination in employment. This encompasses any distinction, exclusion or preference made on the basis of race, colour, religion, political opinion, national extraction, social origin or sex, but does not cover special measures for redressing unfair/unequal treatment of particular groups in the labour market (Article 5(2)).

Pursuant to its national and international obligations, the Government has adopted a National Action Programme for citizens of different ethnic origins. Immigrants have faced major problems in entering the Norwegian labour market. Most often this takes the form of matching jobs to their qualifications and education. Among employers there has been scepticism concerning immigrant workers, mainly due to lack of knowledge of their professional qualifications. Nevertheless the scepticism might well also be based on discrimination. How else to explain the fact that the majority of immigrant workers holds low status jobs, such as cleaners, hotel workers, and so on?

In April 1993 the Government adopted a national programme of action to increase the number of immigrants engaged in gainful employment, mainly by encouraging Norwegian employers to employ immigrant workers. One of the principal goals is to raise employers' awareness of the fact that immigrants have the necessary skill and knowledge to carry out the jobs available. It highlighted where the problem areas were: for immigrant workers, these include insufficient fluency in the national language; insufficient knowledge of the Norwegian labour market; insufficient knowledge of the relevant national legislation; and insufficient knowledge about Norwegian society. On the employers' side, these include unwarranted reservations concerning immigrant workers; discrimination on the basis of ethnicity; and a lack of information about their skills and knowledge. The programme also aims at reducing the obstacles facing immigrant workers in employment by trying to solve some of the problems on both sides.

Special measures in the form of affirmative action for immigrant workers in employment are among the following elements of the programme:

(a) introduction of an approval system for immigrant workers' education and professional qualifications, involving the systematic collection of data on foreign education systems and examinations, tests of immigrant workers' language and professional skills and improving the system for approval of higher education certificates obtained elsewhere;

(b) accelerated language training, including an evaluation of the Norwegian language training system for immigrants;

(c) improving the registration system for the educational and professional qualifications of immigrant workers and better information for immigrants about the Norwegian education system and labour market;

(d) recruitment, with closer contact between the State Labour Market Department/Administration and employers who would like to employ immigrant workers, and the establishment of a system where Norwegians with the same educational background as the immigrants can offer their assistance in settling the immigrants in the labour market; and

(e) creation of new jobs by assisting immigrants in starting their own business through specific courses on how to establish your own business.

By the end of 1993, an average of approximately 9,000 non-native-Norwegian speakers participated in ordinary labour market schemes, representing 5.2 per cent of the average number of participants in such schemes. Almost 700 non-native-Norwegian speakers participated in trainee placement schemes that year, representing 4.9 per cent of the total number of such trainees; and 275 such minority members took part in schemes involving supplementary wages to employers for taking part in such affirmative action measures.[3]

IV. THE IMPACT OF MEASURES IN FAVOUR OF ETHNIC MINORITIES

The National Action Programme's concentration on training and information to better prepare immigrant workers to enter the Norwegian labour market would, at face value, have an expected positive impact on their equality in treatment and occupation. As it also encourages measures to be taken to inform employers about the skills and talents of immigrant workers, and their positive contribution to the Norwegian labour market, it enforces the approach that success of such programmes is based on mutual understanding and knowledge.

However, while few national evaluations on this specific approach are available, it has been demonstrated in other relevant studies that there is still a long way to go in achieving genuine equality in the workforce through special measures. Workers of different ethnic background invariably are highly represented in unemployment figures, still work in low-status jobs and experience little socio-economic mobility. These common conclusions were found for other Western European countries having solid equality legislation and affirmative action programmes including special language and general integration elements similar to those outlined above for Norway.[4] In fact, in Norway, at the end of May 1993 the number of immigrants registered as unemployed was 9,500 or 10.7 per cent of the labour force. It is to be hoped that the special schemes introduced the following year will turn this figure around.

Notes

[1] Norway's report to the Economic and Social Council's Committee on Economic, Social and Cultural Rights, United Nations, 1994a, paras. 64-69.

[2] Minority Rights Group (MRG), 1988; ILO, 1995a, p. 399.

[3] United Nations, 1994a, paras. 72-78.

[4] Zegers de Beijl, 1991, pp. 44-46.

THE PHILIPPINES
Arturo Borjal*

6

In recent years, there have been serious efforts in both the government and non-government sectors to accelerate the integration of the disabled and cultural minorities into the mainstream of social and economic life of the Philippines. This study will focus on affirmative action efforts to overcome discrimination mainly through legislative action, and to a lesser degree through policy statements.

The first part of the study is mainly a review of available documents and materials dealing with the promotion of equal employment opportunities for disabled persons. Selected available data and statistics are presented as indicators of success in the implementation of specific programmes. The second part deals with the employment opportunities for members of the ethnic communities but the discussion is limited by the availability of reliable data from primary sources.

I. PERSONS WITH DISABILITIES

In considering the disability situation, the Philippines uses the International Classification of Impairments, Disabilities and Handicaps (ICIDH) of the World Health Organization (WHO). Thus the terms impairment, disability and handicap are defined as follows:

Impairment. Any loss or abnormality of psychological, physiological or anatomical structure or function. Impairments are disturbances at the level of the organ that include defects or loss of limb, organ or other body structure, as well as defects or loss of mental function. Examples of impairments that have been asked about in censuses and surveys include: blindness, deafness, loss of sight in an eye, paralysis of limb, amputation of limb, mental retardation, partial sight and loss of speech.

Disability. Any restriction or lack (resulting from an impairment) of ability to perform an activity in the manner or within the range considered normal for a human being. This term describes a functional limitation or activity restriction caused by an impairment. Disabilities are descriptions of disturbances in function at the level of the person. Examples of disabilities

---

* Congressman, Philippines Congress.

that have been asked about in censuses and surveys include: difficulty seeing, speaking, hearing, moving, climbing stairs, grasping, reaching, bathing, eating, and using the lavatory.

Handicap. A disadvantage for a given individual, resulting from an impairment or disability, that limits or prevents the fulfilment of a role that is normal (depending on age, sex and social and cultural factors) for that individual. The term is also a classification of "circumstances in which disabled people are likely to find themselves". Handicap describes the social and economic roles of impaired or disabled persons that place them at a disadvantage compared to other persons. These disadvantages are a result of the interaction of the person with specific environments and cultures. Examples of handicaps that have been asked about in censuses or surveys include: bedridden, confined to home, unable to use public transport, not working, underemployed, and socially isolated.

Republic Act No. 7277, otherwise known as the "Magna Carta for Disabled Persons", adopts the ICIDH definition of the above terms verbatim.

The first and only major national disability survey was made in 1980 and published in 1983. An update was done in 1990 but the results were met with scepticism due to the low prevalence rates. Philippine experts assume that the real current prevalence rates of disability are higher than those suggested by the 1980 national disability survey. The benchmark national survey has consistently been less than those cited by focused studies done by experts on specific disability conditions. Thus, the total estimated number of disabled persons was estimated to be 2.68 million in 1990, and was expected to rise to a little over 3 million in 1995. Of the estimated number in 1995, about 2.6 million are expected to be physically impaired, 272,800 are expected to be mentally impaired, and a little over 700,000 will have mixed impairments.

The landmark legislation is Republic Act No. 7277, entitled "An Act Providing for the Rehabilitation, Self-Development and Self-Reliance of Disabled Persons and their Integration into the Mainstream of Society and for other Purposes". Passed by the Eighth Philippine Congress in 1991, it provides for comprehensive measures aimed at ending prejudices and biases against the disabled. It clearly defines the rights and privileges of disabled persons concerning employment, education, health, auxiliary and social services, telecommunications, accessibility, as well as political and civil liberties. It is the most significant piece of local legislation thus far encompassing equalization of opportunities that fulfils the constitutional mandate of equality for all citizens, regardless of status. On the one hand, the Act specifically prohibits discrimination against disabled persons and provides for penalties, including fines and imprisonment, for violations; on the other hand, it grants incentives such as tax privileges to persons and entities supportive of affirmative action programmes and activities in favour of the disabled. In essence, it seeks to remove social barriers present in institutions — whether legal, economic, cultural, or recreational, affecting any human group, community or subdivision of society — which limit the fullest possible participation of disabled persons in the life of the group. It defines social barriers in this context as those negative attitudes that tend to single out and exclude disabled persons and which distort roles and interpersonal relationships.

Of great significance is the recognition that the lofty aims of equalization of opportunities can only be realized if opportunities could be expanded to make the disabled productive members of society through employment. In this respect, the Act provides that no disabled persons shall be denied access to opportunities for suitable employment.

Specific affirmative action measures in the form of a quota appears in section 5, entitled "Equal Opportunity for Employment", which mandates that 5 per cent of a certain class of positions in departments or offices engaged in social development shall be reserved for disabled persons. Section 5 reads:

> No disabled person shall be denied access to opportunities for suitable employment. A qualified disabled employee shall be subject to the same terms and conditions of employment and the same compensation, privileges, benefits, fringe benefits, incentives or allowances as a qualified able-bodied person. Five per cent (5%) of all casual, emergency and contractual positions in the Departments of Social Welfare and Development; Health; Education, Culture and Sports, and other government offices, agencies or corporations engaged in social development shall be reserved for disabled persons.

By way of incentive or encouragement to employers to participate actively in the programme, private entities that employ disabled persons, either as regular employees, apprentices or learners, shall be entitled to additional deductions from their gross income, equivalent to 25 per cent of the total amount paid as salaries and wages to disabled persons (section 8(b)). Private entities that improve or modify their physical facilities for better accommodation of disabled persons shall also be entitled to additional deduction from their net taxable income, to an amount of 50 per cent of the direct costs of the improvements or modifications (section 8(c)).

Section 32 lists the following acts as constituting discrimination in employment on the part of public and private employers with regard to disabled job applicants:

— limiting, segregating, or classifying a disabled job applicant in such a manner that it adversely affects his or her work opportunities;

— using qualification standards, employment tests or other selection criteria that screen out or tend to screen out a disabled person unless such standards, tests or other selection criteria are shown to be job-related for the position in question and are consistent with business necessity;

— utilizing standards, criteria, or methods of administration that (a) have the effect of discrimination on the basis of disability; or (b) perpetuate the discrimination of others who are subject to common administrative control;

— providing less compensation, such as salary, wage or other forms of remuneration and fringe benefits, to a qualified employee, by reason of their disability, than the amount to which a non-disabled person performing the same work is entitled;

— favouring a non-disabled employee over a qualified disabled employee with respect to promotion, training opportunities, study and scholarship grants, solely on account of the latter's disability;

— reassigning or transferring a disabled employee to a job or position he or she cannot perform by reason of their disability;

— dismissing or terminating the services of the disabled employee by reason of the disability unless the employer can prove that they impair the satisfactory performance of the work involved to the prejudice of the business entity; provided, however, that the employer first sought to provide reasonable accommodation for disabled persons;

— failing to select or administer in the most effective manner employment tests which accurately reflect skills, aptitude, or other factors of the disabled employee that such tests purport to measure, rather than the impaired sensory, manual or speaking skills of such applicant or employee;

— excluding disabled persons from membership in labour unions or similar organizations.

Under section 44 of the Magna Carta for Disabled Persons, it is the duty of the Secretary of Justice to investigate alleged violations of the Act including its anti-discrimination and quota system provisions, and to undertake periodic reviews of compliance. It is further provided that if the Secretary has reasonable cause to believe that there are persons engaged in a pattern of discrimination or that an act of discrimination raises an issue of general public importance, he or she may commence legal action in any appropriate court. In ordinary terms, this means that a violation of any of the provisions of the Magna Carta is not simply a discriminatory act against a private person but is a crime against the State as well, with the entire prosecutory apparatus of the Government arrayed against the violator. In reality, it is up to the individual discriminated against in violation of the law to bring the case for litigation by filing a complaint before the Justice Department.

Section 45 empowers the courts to grant any equitable relief that it considers appropriate for discrimination cases such as the grant of temporary, preliminary or permanent relief; or, by providing auxiliary aid or service, modification of policy, practice or procedure, or alternative method; or by making facilities readily accessible to and usable by disabled persons.

The quota scheme to reserve a certain percentage of positions for the disabled initially met with resistance during the legislative deliberations, not so much because of the complexities of enforcing the quota on the employers, but rather because of the fundamental belief that persons, disabled or not, should be employed on the basis of their own skills and proficiencies and not by special dispensation. The conventional wisdom was that people with disabilities should compete in the job market on their own merits. Nevertheless, and in recognition of the inherent limitations that prevent the disabled from realizing their full potential, a compromise was reached such that the law in its final form took the shape of a half measure, in the sense that the quota scheme was applied only to certain government departments and not to private employers. Data are not available on whether government departments covered by the scheme have complied fully with the law's mandate to reserve positions for people with disabilities and reports on compliance are still being awaited for proper evaluation. In the end, the success of the mandatory scheme will depend to a large degree on the success of the parallel positive measures such as rehabilitation and training which will give people with disabilities the necessary skills to integrate into the labour force without resort to coercive quota measures.

Impetus for implementation might be forthcoming following the signing, on 15 January 1993, of Proclamation No. 125. This provides for the nationwide observance of the Asian and Pacific Decade of Disabled Persons, from 1993 to 2002, and directs all instrumentalities of the national Government, NGOs, self-help groups and professional associations to develop and implement programmes that will promote the equalization of opportunities for the disabled persons to upgrade their living standards.

Other regulatory provisions supporting affirmative action in this area include the Philippine Constitution. In Article XIII, section 13, it directs the establishment of a special agency for disabled persons for their rehabilitation, self-development and self-reliance. This agency shall also be asked to work out programmes for the integration of the disabled in the mainstream of society.

Book 11, Chapter 11, of the Labour Code contains a prohibition of the curtailment of employment opportunities for disabled persons.

The State Insurance Fund Act lays down conditions for remuneration for injury or illness of an employee. Expanded categories of employers who are required to give disability remuneration are also included. A corollary to this is the Employees' Compensation Chapter of the Labour Code which stipulates that injured employees shall be entitled to medical services during the subsequent period of this disability through the system that covers them (social security system or government service insurance system).

The Vocational Rehabilitation Act provides for the establishment of rehabilitation workshops for the disabled with the involvement of the private sector.

Memorandum Circular No. 37 (series of 1990) was issued by the Civil Service Commission to provide for mechanisms for disabled persons (crippled, deaf, mute or blind and persons who suffer partial disability) to apply for and take the civil service examinations. Moreover, these disabled persons who pass the examinations shall be issued with the prescribed certificates of eligibility. In addition, resolution No. 11 (1990) was passed by the National Council for the Welfare of the Disabled. It requests all examination administering boards and government agencies issuing licences to allow disabled persons to take board or civil service examinations and to be issued with all types of licences made available to non-disabled persons. However, inquiries with the Civil Service Commission's Office for Recruitment Examination and Placement (OREP) showed that from 1989 to 1994 only about 30 individuals had applied to sit the examinations.

A concrete positive measure recently adopted merits special mention: "Tulay 2000" (Tulong, Alalay Sa Taong May Kapansanan Help and Aid to Handicapped People) was launched on 21 February 1994 as a series of special training and employment programmes for persons with disabilities. The Department of Labor and Employment and the Department of Welfare and Social Development are the main agents for its implementation. It involves four programme components: (a) an inventory of skills of persons with disabilities, (b) training programmes to prepare persons with disabilities for employment, to cover industrial skills, livelihood skills, and entrepreneurship skills; (c) wage employment (qualified persons with disabilities are referred to private companies and government agencies where job vacancies are available for them); and (d) self-employment (financial and technical assistance are also extended to such persons in coordination with NGOs and government livelihood agencies).

At various stages when Tulay 2000 was being drawn up, representatives from NGOs representing persons with disabilities were consulted (such as the National Council for the Welfare of Disabled Persons, National Manpower and Youth Council, Bureau of Disabled Persons Welfare, Technology and Livelihood Resource Center, Tahanang Walang Hagdanan and Employees' Compensation Commission). Additionally, and in order to promote and encourage the participation of the employers' sector in the employment of persons with disability, the initiators of the programme coordinate closely with various industry groups, including local government units. The Bureau of Local Employment (BLE), a line agency under the Department of Labor and Employment, has already selected pilot areas for the initial implementation of Tulay 2000. The BLE as of June 1994 conducted a survey of 1,000 companies and establishments in the National Capital Region, to identify employment opportunities available to qualified persons with disabilities in the wage sector. Of 1,000 respondents, 15 firms gave a positive response and signified interest in hiring qualified persons with disabilities over the next five years. A limited effort has also been attempted by the BLE to monitor and verify their actual employment in various establishments.

II. PROBLEMS AND RECOMMENDATIONS

There is inadequate information, especially statistical data, to indicate the number of persons with disabilities who have been employed in the past in the wage sector, or are currently employed in both the government service and in the private sector. Moreover, there are no data on the skills which may be considered in demand in so far as they are concerned to match the current job market requirements. These data could help define strategies for training and rehabilitation of persons with disabilities. A more active advocacy and information campaign to heighten public awareness on the need to create employment opportunities for such persons should be initiated, implemented and sustained.

Training and rehabilitation programmes for persons with disabilities should be conceptualized, implemented in collaboration with industries and establishments that have actual need for their skills and services, to facilitate eventual absorption of qualified disabled persons in the job market.

A system for monitoring the outcome and results of programmes initiated for these groups should be in place to serve as a basis for future plans and projects for them.

III. ETHNIC MINORITIES

In the Philippine context, the term "ethnic minorities" is used interchangeably with the terms national minorities, cultural minorities, ethnic groups or aboriginal and indigenous cultural communities — all referring to "a group of people sharing common bonds of language, customs, tradition and other distinctive cultural traits, and who have since time immemorial occupied, possessed and utilized a territory". This appears to be the operative definition among development planners in government who formulated it within the framework of the Comprehensive Agrarian Reform Act and the Act Providing for the Establishment and Management of a National Integrated Protected Areas System (NIPAS).

The first inhabitants of the Philippines were pygmies, ancestors of what are now known as negritoes, who crossed the ancient and now submerged land bridges that linked the islands to the Asian mainland. In separate migratory waves by sea, they were followed by Malaya-Polynesian migrants from various parts of South-East Asia. They created communities and flourished for centuries until the Spaniards came and subjugated the inhabitants, save for a few groups who withdrew into the interior. Those who embraced Spanish rule and Christianity became the majority while those who resisted retained their indigenous identity and became the cultural minorities.

Ethnic minorities are to be found throughout the islands, comprising about 60 distinct tribes. Their total population is estimated to be about 12 to 13 million, or about 18 per cent of the whole population as of 1991. Of this number, 5 million are Muslims. A partial list of the main groups, their settlement areas and numbers is as follows:

Maguindanao	Mindanao and Palawan	1 900 000
Maranao	Mindanao and Palawan	1 500 000
Ibanag	Isabela, Cagayan	1 105 000
Tausug	Mindanao and Palawan	800 000
Yakan/Samal	Mindanao provinces	800 000
Manobo	Mindanao provinces	600 000
B'laan	Mindanao provinces	370 000

Indigenous peoples subsist mainly by hunting, fishing and gathering of forest products aside from farming. In recent years these activities have become decreasingly productive as the country's resources continue to dwindle. Most of these groups produce clothing materials, household goods and utensils, and simple farm tools, engaging in pottery, textile and basket weaving, carving, breadmaking, dyeing and metalwork. Items not produced in the household or village are obtained through barter. Other economic activities include farming as tenants and hiring out as labour for mines, logging operations, or plantations.

In the main, government assistance to the ethnic minorities to provide employment consists of livelihood projects along the lines of their traditional economic activities. The Department of Trade and Industry (DTI) project described below is one such assistance programme.

Prime movers in the national approach to ethnic development are the three government offices — Office for Northern Cultural Communities (ONCC), Office for Southern Cultural Communities (OSCC) and Office on Muslim Affairs (OMA) — which were created immediately after the 1986 revolution. Attached to the Office of the President, their task is to preserve and develop the culture, traditions and institutions of the cultural communities and to promote their well-being in consonance with national unity and development. They are mandated to promote the enactment of laws and regulations concerning indigenous communities' rights to their ancestral lands, provide medical assistance and nutrition services, promote livelihood projects, issue certificates of tribal memberships for benefits provided under the law, coordinate all developmental activities implemented by other governmental agencies in areas inhabited by indigenous communities, and advise the President in formulation of policies for these peoples. Despite this broad mandate, the Offices function primarily as intermediate bodies between indigenous communities seeking assistance and the concerned line departments, due in large part to financial constraints. As far as can be ascertained, some programmes that these agencies are implementing do have employment or vocational training elements, but only as far as these elements form an integral part of primarily livelihood projects. The minuscule budgets of these agencies severely limit the impact of whatever employment or vocational training programmes are being implemented, if any.

Operational activities and the actual implementation of the different programmes and projects to improve the livelihood of indigenous peoples are funded through very limited resources released by the Budget Department on a project-by-project basis, or allocations disbursed through members of Congress. Serious attempts have been made to rationalize all programmes into a cohesive plan but as yet there is no discernible affirmative action employment strategy to promote the employment of these groups.

At the legislature level, a Committee on Indigenous Cultural Communities exists to consider Bills concerning these communities, but so far its performance has been weak.

More recently, the National Committee on the International Year for the World's Indigenous People was established. It is chaired by the Department of Foreign Affairs and the Department of Energy and Natural Resources and comprises 14 governmental agencies including the major departments. Its activities so far have been mainly promotional and awareness-raising in character. Worthy of note is its draft joint resolution urging the creation of a congressional commission to undertake a comprehensive assessment of the conditions of indigenous communities and review all relevant laws and policies.

There are now two major national indigenous federations, namely KAMP (National Federation of Indigenous Peoples in the Philippines) and TRICAP, and a number of scattered local and regional organizations. TRICAP works closely with the Government in several initiatives concerning indigenous communities while KAMP is linked closely with the international network supporting indigenous causes worldwide. Coming together for the first time in 1993 during the ILO-sponsored events related to the ILO's Indigenous and Tribal Peoples Convention, 1989 (No. 169), the two groups set aside their political differences and discussed their major problems.

Among the indigenous and tribal peoples, various types of cooperatives have been established in cooperation with government agencies such as the Cooperative Development Authority and the OMA, ONCC and OSCC. Many NGOs are also working at the grass-roots level to help the indigenous peoples to set up cooperatives. In the Cordillera region alone, 597 primary cooperatives were registered in 1991. In Visayas and Mindanao, the OSCC field offices assisted tribal communities in establishing 22 cooperatives in 1991 and ten cooperatives in 1992.

A number of Bills dealing with indigenous cultural communities have been considered in both houses of Congress but none has been enacted so far. Of particular interest is Senate Bill No. 153 aimed at ensuring equal employment opportunities to Muslims and tribal Filipinos, and Bill No. 212 which provides for equal employment opportunities in all offices, agencies or branches of government to members of cultural communities and the allotment of at least 15 per cent of all positions to the members of the indigenous communities. As far as can be ascertained there has been no case filed in the courts involving discrimination — not because discrimination is non-existent, but because there is simply no law upon which to build a case.

Article II, section 22, of the Philippine Constitution declares it state policy to recognize and promote the rights of indigenous cultural minorities within the framework of national unity and development. In line with this policy, government agencies such as the above-mentioned OSCC, ONCC and OMA were created.

Under present policy, members of the cultural minorities may take liberalized civil service examinations in recognition of the economic and social factors that prevent them from meeting the standard pass marks and from competing favourably with others.

Current available data furnished by the Bureau of Local Employment Statistics (BLES) do not show information on the number of members of ethnic minorities who are actually employed.

There are programmes implemented by the Department of Trade and Industry (DTI) for registered tribal communities. The project components vary by tribal group and do not necessarily include areas of assistance, as follows: registration of rural workers' associations; rehabilitation and livelihood programmes through financial assistance; conduct of seminars and training (vocational skills training, entrepreneurship, organizational management and capability, and farming). The beneficiaries of these DTI initiated projects have been: 672 residents from Mt. Pinatubo areas; 2,473 in the Cordillera Administrative Region; and some 20 upland farmers from the Manobo Tribe Economic Development Association in Ormoc City. For the livelihood projects started for the Manobos in Ormoc City, no evaluation report or data are available at present to indicate how the project is progressing. The same applies to the Mt. Pinatubo programme recipients. The rehabilitation programme and corresponding monetary aid can be identified, but the available reports are not sufficient to gauge the success of these efforts at the moment. In the Cordillera Administrative Region, livelihood initiatives were financed through a combination of loans and grants to various tribal groups. As of August 1994, some eight projects through loan funds were terminated, ten projects through loan funds are ongoing and four projects made possible through grants are continuing. The longest running project in this region, which started in 1989 through loan funds and continues to date, is known as the WEED project and is engaged in citrus and hog production.

IV. PROBLEMS AND RECOMMENDATIONS

The non-availability of reliable information and statistical data on the total recipients of government and non-government initiated affirmative action programmes for the tribal communities in the country severely limits the quantification of the direct impact of such programmes in the socio-economic uplifting of these groups. A comprehensive study to cover these aspects should be conducted. The resulting data should be able to help planners define approaches and programmes that will address the priority concerns for these groups to integrate them into the mainstream of society.

THE RUSSIAN FEDERATION
A.A. Tkachenko,*
A.V. Koryukhina** and T.V. Matveeva**

7

I. THE EMPLOYMENT SITUATION OF DISABLED PERSONS

Persons with disabilities are one of the least protected and, hence, most vulnerable groups in the labour market. Because of the special nature of the disabled workforce, a special approach must be adopted to problems relating to their employment. In this regard, the Vocational Rehabilitation and Employment (Disabled Persons) Convention (No. 159), which was ratified by the Russian Federation on 3 June 1988, has been the benchmark used when the Government draws up its policy in the field of employment of persons with disabilities.

Many unemployed disabled persons want to work. Regional surveys conducted in 1992 and 1993 indicate that 21 per cent of unemployed disabled persons expressed an unconditional desire to participate in working life, nearly 29 per cent would like to work in certain circumstances, and only about half surveyed indicated that they did not wish to participate in the labour force. The main reason cited by disabled people for unemployment was poor health (30.4 per cent of those surveyed) and the unwillingness of employers to hire disabled people (12 per cent).

The number of disabled people registered with social protection bodies in Russia and receiving disability pensions was 4.2 million on 1 January 1994, a figure based on the count of people disabled as a result of general illness, industrial injuries or occupational illnesses, military service and those disabled since birth. In actual fact, the number of disabled people in the country is about twice as high, as disabled people who receive old-age pensions and survivors' benefits and who are registered with other departments (such as the Ministry of Defence or the Ministry of Internal Affairs and Security) are not taken into account in these statistics. At the beginning of 1993, 663,000 disabled people, or about 20 per cent of the

* Director, Labour Market Policy and Population Department, Ministry of Labour, Russian Federation.
** Officials of the same Department.

overall number, were employed in the Russian Federation. Since 1991, there has been a reduction in both absolute and relative terms in the number of disabled workers.

In Russia there are differences in demand for disabled workers within the labour market. Studies have shown that many disabled people need vocational training and job placement services. Vocational rehabilitation for disabled people currently satisfies only 15 per cent of demand, and nearly 50 per cent of disabled workers occupy posts that are not suited to them. What is more, few disabled people who use job placement services succeed in finding a job. In 1993 some 26,600 persons in receipt of disability pensions turned to the labour and employment services in search of job placement. This accounted for 1.2 per cent of all jobseekers. Unfortunately, it is not possible to discern long-term trends in the formation of a labour market for disabled workers; data on the placement of disabled people seeking employment were not available until 1993. But one element is clear. During the period of market transformation, the employment situation of many of the most vulnerable social groups, including disabled persons, has worsened.

The employment problems facing disabled people in the Russian Federation are indeed complex. However, society has begun to take a new look at the problems of disability. A new concept is gaining ground, one in which persons with disabilities are integrated into society and are related to as people capable of being educated and trained, of working, of earning a living, of having an active life of leisure and of fulfilling themselves in the fields of science, culture and art, and one in which they are members of society in conditions of equality in practice, and not just in theory. In this context, it is not so much material assistance in the form of benefits or privileges that is needed, but rather vocational and social rehabilitation in line with the expectations of the disabled themselves.

Legislative measures

As for specific positive measures on behalf of persons with disabilities, a major step was taken in 1993 with the adoption of Decree No. 394 on measures for the vocational rehabilitation and provision for the employment of persons with disabilities. It contains a series of measures to encourage the employment of disabled people and defines who is responsible for each measure and sets a time-frame for its implementation. It recognizes the usefulness of establishing recruitment quotas at enterprises and organizations of all forms of ownership, and calls for the introduction of mandatory payments to the State Employment Fund of the Russian Federation for enterprises and organizations not fulfilling these quotas. State employment bodies must establish specialized groups for the vocational rehabilitation and employment of disabled individuals.

The Decree obliges a number of ministries and departments, beginning in 1993, "to organize, in the training institutes that fall within their competence, vocational training and retraining programmes for the disabled, first and foremost for professions and specialities which will make disabled people as competitive as possible in the regional labour markets".

The Decree advises local executive bodies to take the following positive measures:

— to conduct preferential financial and credit policies to make possible the establishment of specialized enterprises and organizations which hire disabled persons, and to provide budgetary financing for the creation of special posts;

— to assist in restoring the financial and economic health of special enterprises which employ disabled workers;

— to provide general support and assistance to enterprises and organizations which assume responsibility for the occupational rehabilitation of persons with disabilities and the provision of employment for disabled workers;

— to make use of extra-budgetary resources for the financing of occupational rehabilitation activities and the provision of employment for disabled persons; and

— to foster the extension of home work for persons with disabilities.

Federal programmes

To implement this Decree, the Federal Employment Service, together with the ministries and departments concerned, has drawn up a federal programme of vocational rehabilitation and employment for 1994, which defines the aims and priorities of government policy in the field of vocational rehabilitation and employment of persons with disabilities. Its main aim is to create conditions so that the potential capabilities of disabled persons may be used in the labour market, by providing vocational guidance, vocational training, appropriate placement and increased incentives for employers, so as to help solve the problems of employment for the disabled. The measures it foresees include:

— the establishment of a vocational rehabilitation system;

— social assistance for persons with disabilities who are unemployed, and for disabled people with disabled children;

— the training of supervisory staff to carry out vocational rehabilitation;

— the revision of the legal standards and methodological basis for the vocational rehabilitation of persons with disabilities, and the provision of employment for them;

— the provision of scientific support to help solve the problems of vocational rehabilitation and employment;

— the creation and maintenance of posts for persons with disabilities;

— the provision of wage subsidies for disabled persons;

— the maintenance of posts at special enterprises; and

— the fostering of self-employment of disabled people and support for persons with disabilities who engage in entrepreneurial activities.

In practice there are currently several basic approaches to tackling the problem of employment of disabled people. These include the use of quotas for disabled workers in the mainstream in ordinary enterprises (whereby it is possible to reserve a number of posts for disabled persons), the use of disabled workers in special enterprises and the creation of new posts for disabled workers.

Often, disabled persons can be employed in the "special enterprises" (special work) of the various federal government departments. At the beginning of 1993, some 77,000 disabled people were employed in 1,445 special enterprises in Russia, representing 26 per cent of the overall number of workers at these enterprises. The majority of these workers were employed at home (30 per cent of the disabled workers) and in part-time jobs (21 per cent of the disabled workers).

Disabled persons are rarely employed in public works. Staff at employment centres have noted that unemployed people in general, and disabled people in particular, are very reluctant to take part in public works. Participation in public works lacks prestige and is poorly paid. It is essential to give some thought to the setting up and implementation of public works programmes so that they have more status and better wage levels and conditions of work. For young disabled workers, public works must create the conditions for their further advancement and must provide them with a stronger vocational occupational orientation (for example, in medical institutions or postal organizations).

Other federal programmes, while not dealing specifically with employment issues, impact on the employment of persons with disabilities. For example, the Ministry of Social Protection has elaborated an overall federal programme for the scientific support and computerization of work related to disabilities and disabled persons, for the period from 1994 to 1997. The main aim of this programme is to reduce the adverse effects of the social and economic changes on the status of the disabled in Russia by implementing a coordinated set of measures of an organizational, scientific and practical nature, such as elaborating guiding principles with reference to the social, economic and legal aspects of providing social services for disabled persons; ensuring that disabled persons can live and work independently in an accessible environment; fostering the use of computers, forecasting and modelling to ascertain the labour force situation of persons with disabilities in market conditions; and developing a federal programme (for the period from 1994 to 2003) to establish accessible living and working environments for disabled people through a barrier-free architectural environment, the establishment of public and individual passenger transport suitable for disabled people, the introduction of standards for means of communication and computer technologies as well as for everyday services, and decisions in principle concerning the establishment of employment posts for disabled individuals.

The question of the financing of some of these programmes has still not been clarified. It is entirely possible, owing to financial resource limitations, that several will only be partially financed. At the same time, many experts agree that it is imperative for the Government and the Parliament to reconsider their priorities in making decisions about social spending, the environment and investment programmes so as to solve problems related to the improved access of the disabled to the labour force.

II. THE SITUATION OF ETHNIC AND NATIVE MINORITIES

Russia is one of the most ethnically diverse States in the world. The 1989 census delimited 128 separate peoples living in the national territory, not counting a number of small ethnic groups. The largest ethnic groups in Russia are Russians, Tatars, Ukrainians, Chuvash, Bashkirs and Belorussians. They account for some 91 per cent of the total population of Russia.

A national (or ethnic) minority is defined as part of the ethnic whole living beyond the borders of its territory of traditional settlement and in another national environment, but which maintains its culture, traditions or simply its ethnic identity. Until recently, the population of Russia was becoming increasingly mixed. Moreover, for ideological reasons it was considered a single nation. It was particularly difficult in such an environment to elaborate a national policy acknowledging such multicultural diversities.

After 1917, state policies concerning nationality led to an administrative division of the country along national lines. Of the over 100 nationalities in Russia, 38 currently have national territorial formations of some kind — republics or autonomous regions *(okrugs* or *oblasts),* the borders of which generally correspond with the regions where these ethnic groups predominate. None the less, these formations have a rather complex ethnic composition. Because of the centuries-old mixing of the population, large groups of these populations may, in many cases, live outside the borders of their main territories of settlement. Consequently, if they maintain their culture, traditions or ethnic identity, they may be defined for these territories as national or ethnic minorities.

After 1991, with the fall of the USSR and the removal of the state control concerning questions of nationality, separatist movements began to develop, with a rise in ethnic tensions. Attempts were made to claim a preemptive right of access to natural resources for the "entitled" nationalities in the republics and to give them precedence in the political and cultural institutions, to the detriment of the non-indigenous population. A decisive measure in this regard was the introduction in a number of autonomous regions of an official state language. This led to the worsening of inter-ethnic relations. It also prompted the accelerated departure of various nationalities from the autonomous regions and republics, where these laws began to infringe upon the civil and employment rights of these people. The accelerating drop in production during the economic transformation only worsened the situation. It first affected the non-indigenous populations and ethnic minorities. With the rapid deterioration in living and working conditions many non-indigenous specialists are leaving the republics and autonomous regions of Siberia and the far east.

Regarding the native peoples of the north, who are few in number, they have a special place in the social and economic structure of society. In Russia, they are defined as groups with fewer than 50,000 members, who live in the territory of traditional settlement of their ancestors and who maintain an everyday way of life and an identity as a separate people. There are 61 ethnic groups that are considered small, indigenous, native peoples; their overall population is slightly more than 440,000 (or 0.3 per cent of the population). Of these groups, six are located in the European part of Russia, 22 in the northern Caucasus and 33 in the north, in Siberia or in the far east. These small native peoples have the same rights as all citizens of Russia. However, their small numbers make their integration into the social and economic structure of an industrial society difficult. They are particularly vulnerable because of the economic and social development of the territories where they live and the inability to adapt their way of life and values to the market now taking shape in Russia and to the special demands of the transitional period.

Special attention, albeit sometimes misguided, has thus historically been given to the small native peoples of the north. In the mid-1930s, efforts made (sometimes on a forced basis) to include them in the economic life of the country and to make nomadic or semi-nomadic peoples settle were often implemented without taking into consideration the specific way of life, family make-up and traditions or origins of these peoples. The end result was that the traditional economic systems, the basis on which these peoples survived, were destroyed.

Organizational structures

In the late 1980s and early 1990s, during the period of perestroika, a number of regional and countrywide organizations were established to defend the interests of native peoples. More than 11 public organizations are registered with the Ministry of Justice, and in the regional duma (local parliament) of the Khanty-Mansi Autonomous Region there is a special form of ethnic representation; it is composed of an assembly of representatives of the small native peoples of the north. Elsewhere, similar associations have a right of legislative initiative and their opinion is taken into consideration when decisions are made which affect their interests. Their role in the monitoring of hiring of manpower among small minority populations is defined in the regulations for the activities of associations. Financial structures for the revival of numerically small native peoples have also been established (including the Fund for the Revival of Small Native Peoples, the Survival Fund). These can assist in the re-establishment of production activities in traditional sectors of employment. None the less, this work has not been carried out effectively or sufficiently because of the limited resources available.

Legislative measures

The legislative background for affirmative action to redress the employment situation of ethnic and native minorities is endorsed in international treaties. The Russian Federation adheres strictly to the basic provisions of the United Nations Universal Declaration of Human Rights, the ILO's Discrimination (Employment and Occupation) Convention, 1958 (No. 111), and other international instruments which forbid discrimination in the field of labour and employment based on national characteristics or ethnic origin.

At the national level, the All-Russian Central Executive Committee and the Council of People's Commissars issued a Decree in 1926 on the establishment of temporary provisions concerning the management of indigenous nationalities and tribes of the northern parts of the then RSFSR. It gave native peoples a special status, provided they met certain criteria: a small population, the special nature of their traditional economic system (based on reindeer breeding, hunting or fishing), a nomadic or semi-nomadic lifestyle, a particular cultural way of life and a low level of social and economic development. These criteria are still used today.

The Constitution of the Russian Federation (article 69) guarantees the rights of numerically small indigenous peoples in accordance with generally recognized principles and standards of international law and with the international treaties of the Russian Federation. The Employment Act of 1990 guarantees equal opportunities for all citizens living in the national territory, regardless of, inter alia, nationality (in the sense of national extraction) in the exercise of their right to work and to choose freely their employment. It also ensures that there is employment for numerically small native peoples and nationalities of Russia where they live, taking into account the characteristics of their economic and cultural activities and the types of employment that have historically been prevalent among them.

Other newly adopted statutes deal with elements of the employment situation of numerically small native peoples: the Act on State Guarantees and Compensation for People Working and Living in the Regions of the Far North and Similar Regions (of particular interest as it grants special pension entitlements for people living in these regions and working as reindeer breeders, fishermen or commercial hunters); the Land Code; the Basic Principles of Forestry Legislation; the Act on Mineral Reserves; the Act on the Privatization of State and Municipal Enterprises (which grants them preferential treatment in taking over traditional craft enterprises at their residual cost); the Education Act; and the Income Tax Act.

In addition, since late 1994 the State Duma (the lower house of parliament) has been considering a bill on the legal status of numerically small native peoples of Russia. The ILO has provided technical input to the parliamentary debate. This far-reaching text, which draws inspiration from the 1966 International Convention on the Elimination of All Forms of Racial Discrimination and the ILO's Indigenous and Tribal Peoples Convention,

1989 (No. 169), is mainly aimed at governing property rights for land and other natural resources, compensation for damages caused to the environment in the territories in which such peoples live, state support and assistance in continuing traditional economic activities, and self-government and the representation of native peoples in bodies with responsibility for providing employment (namely local self-government bodies). It calls for special vocational training programmes, taking into consideration the special nature of the traditional economy. Finally, it reserves seats at certain educational establishments at the secondary and higher levels.

Shortcomings in the proposed legislation are that it does not extend to non-traditional sectors of the economy and that it does not contain a precise implementation procedure, nor indicate which authority is responsible for implementation. Moreover, since the only framework dealing specifically with the hiring and employment of people from native groups is the legislation concerning the activities of native peoples' associations, it would be useful, on the basis of international experience, to develop further mechanisms and legal standards for recruitment and the activities of employment agencies in relation to these peoples so that affirmative action in their favour in this domain has a solid legal basis. Part of the improved framework should include better local information systems for the native peoples so that they are kept informed of their rights in the labour legislation and of the means to defend those rights.

Federal programmes

In addition to the legislative programme, in March 1991 the Government adopted a programme for the economic and cultural development of native peoples of the north, for the period from 1991 to 1995. However, the severe economic crisis and the political changes that have taken place in the country have had an extremely adverse effect on the financing and implementation of this programme, in particular the elements that were supposed to create housing, social and cultural facilities and production capacity.

The provision of special positive measures favouring the economic development of Russia's northern native peoples cannot be considered without reference to the problems these groups have faced in education and vocational training related to their traditional employment patterns. Until the beginning of 1992, the number of economically active members of the minority peoples of the north steadily increased. In the period 1981-91, the number of manual workers, white-collar workers and collective farm workers from these groups increased by an average of 22.6 per cent in practically all occupations. As the transition to a market economy began, the number of indigenous people in employment began to fall. In 1992 alone, their number fell by almost 10 per cent. This has affected 21 of the 26 northern peoples. The largest reductions in employment levels were among Inuit (-30.9 per cent), Chukchi (-28.6 per cent), Saami (-22.1 per cent) and Itelmen (-19.5 per cent).

The main reasons for this fall in employment levels are the reduction in the numbers of reindeer kept, owing to the reorganization of collective and state farms, reductions in fish-processing factories because of dwindling fish stocks, the closure of forestry plantations, the sharp fall in investment in industrial construction, and the commercialization of trade and catering; most of the jobs lost as a result of the latter were unskilled ones, which were generally occupied by members of the native peoples of the north.

Moreover, this reduction in the numbers of indigenous people in employment is taking place at a time when the potential working population is increasing. As a result, as many as 25-30 per cent of potential workers from the minority peoples of the north are to all intents and purposes unemployed and earn a living only by gathering wild plants, fishing, hunting and small-scale reindeer herding. According to a specially conducted survey, almost 15 per cent of those capable of work do not wish to work. The unemployment rate among young people and women is especially high. For instance, 83 per cent of unemployed Evenks in Amurskaya Oblast (a medium-sized administrative area) are women.

Some of the problems involved in finding jobs for the native people of the north are partly due to their unwillingness to move to other areas. A sociological survey showed that 20 per cent of the non-native population would seek work outside their own region if they lost their jobs. However, only 2 per cent of the native population were prepared to do the same. Even this figure may be too high, since the vast majority of indigenous people who leave their place of permanent residence later return there, having become marginalized in the new place. Moreover, in Krasnoyarskij Kraj (a large administrative area), more than 90 per cent of respondents to the survey believed that their lives should continue to be based on traditional occupations.

As the Russian economy adapts to market principles, more and more new forms of organization of production and employment are appearing in the traditional occupations of the peoples of the north — farms, communal/clan farm businesses and small family enterprises and cooperatives. Many new independent businesses are being set up as part of the reorganization of collective and state farms; although they are called by many different names, there are no fundamental differences in the way they are organized. Essentially, they mark a return to the traditional family- and clan-based activities of the indigenous peoples, in a new form based on individual and collective forms of ownership and regulating their own family and labour relationships. At the same time, without the regulating hand of the State — from the federal down to the local level — it would be impossible for them to gain an easy and successful entry into the new economy.

According to minority peoples' organizations and the relevant state agencies — the Ministry of Nationality Affairs and Regional Policy and the committees of the State Duma — the question of land rights and land use is crucial to the resolution of the labour and employment problems of minority peoples. A Presidential Decree on urgent measures to defend the dwelling places and economic activities of the minority peoples of the north was adopted on 22 April 1992. Considerable attention is paid to this issue in the above-mentioned federal laws such as the Land Code, which regulates the areas where indigenous people live and engage in economic activity and allocates parcels of land for reindeer herding and livestock grazing for a temporary period of up to 25 years. It also provides for the possibility of using land which has been designated as protected (for example as a nature reserve) for the purposes of grazing reindeer and hunting, exempts enterprises run by citizens engaged in traditional pursuits from the obligation to pay for the land they use, and states that the peoples concerned shall be consulted about any proposal to use an area of land for purposes unconnected with their economic activities.

Other positive measures outside the legislative ambit include the granting of pasture land and hunting and fishing grounds practically free of charge to members of minority peoples of the north, particularly clan communities, for life or in perpetuity. The land may not be used for purposes unconnected with traditional occupations without their consent.

Another specific problem facing equal employment opportunities for these peoples, and which has been the subject of affirmative action of various kinds in their favour, is their access to vocational education and training. During the pre-reform period there was a massive exodus of people from the northern regions, resulting in jobs requiring qualified specialists being left empty with no prospect of their being filled, since the local indigenous population did not possess the necessary qualifications. For example, of the indigenous population of the north aged over 15 years, 48 per cent have attended primary and some years of secondary school, and 16.9 per cent have not even completed their primary education; almost half the latter are completely illiterate. The low level of general education of indigenous people makes it impossible for them to enter modern professions and ensures that they remain employed, as a rule, in unskilled physical work and in temporary seasonal jobs.

In view of the preponderance of unfilled jobs, two types of training have been developed in order to increase the potential of minority peoples: training of qualified workers for the development of traditional industries; and training of qualified workers for industry, construction and other occupations, taking into account the demands of the indigenous northern peoples themselves, and the need to preserve and develop the existing economic structure and to create local construction bases and processing plants.

The Education Act, which guarantees minority rights, provides for the introduction of state standards for education, consisting of federal and nationality/regional components. It states that pupils may receive their basic general education in their native language. However, in practice there are shortcomings. Since the in-family/community method of passing on traditional skills has been lost, any attempt to "fix" that experience (studying and describing tribal methods of controlling a herd, making use of particular pastures, fattening the livestock, improving fertility, selection, etc.) and pass it on in the context of the modern school or the modern system of industrial training will require the preparation of reference material for every individual region. Experience has shown that training, especially in the case of reindeer herders, can only be successful if it refers to specific conditions and specific areas and if farming and indigenous cultural skills are taught directly. Hence it will be necessary to change the present structure of teaching with a view to devising specific teaching curricula and methods.

The same approach should be taken to the vocational training system. The unique characteristics of indigenous peoples should be taken fully into account in the process of career guidance for members of native nationalities, evaluation of job potential and suitability, and subsequent placement in a job. There are already encouraging signs that sensitization to their skills and talents is happening: networks of small mobile schools, based as closely as possible to the parents' place of work and with a teaching schedule which matches work schedules, are receiving support; the "Children of the North" programme, which is a major component of the federation-wide "Children of Russia" programme, has been warmly received. A further positive programme measure is the proposal to establish centres for young people providing careers guidance, vocational training and job placement following the model "school — specialized secondary school — employment service for school leavers". However, because of cuts in financing, this programme is at present frozen. Another is the Russian/French "Polar Academy" educational establishment, set up at the initiative of the Ministry of Nationality Affairs and Regional Policy, the Ministry of Education and the Government of the Republic of Sakha (Yakutia), with the active participation of the Government of France. It has a special budget to train highly qualified specialists, capable of managing various programmes in the areas of culture, education and management of socio-economic processes in the northern regions in the light of the new economic conditions. An average of 860 students from 18 minority peoples of the north will be trained, and the involved ministries will consider proposals to give members of other minority peoples, particularly the peoples of Dagestan (northern Caucasus), the opportunity to study there. However, in the present economic conditions, it is becoming harder and harder to train specialists from among local people. Because of high transport and living costs, many parents cannot even afford to send their children to secondary school. The only other free special study places for minority peoples are confined to the Faculty for Minority Peoples of the North at the Herzen Pedagogical University in St. Petersburg. There is also a programme of work rehabilitation for minority peoples at a time of socio-economic change currently being drawn up by the Ministry of Labour in collaboration with the Ministry of Nationality Affairs and Regional Policy, which will aim at finding appropriate employment for trained members of these groups on a preferential basis.

III. CONCLUSIONS

In the preparation and implementation of state work and employment policies for the native peoples of the northern regions of the country, it is essential to develop a range of measures (from appropriate legislation and federal and regional programmes to specific organizational and management decisions) for the establishment of a special system to regulate the labour market and labour relations for these groups. Such a system should ensure the smooth adaptation of ethnic and national communities to the new economic and working conditions, and should give them not only equal employment rights but also, most importantly, a guarantee of social protection in the case of unemployment, as well as promoting the development of their work potential.

UGANDA
Christine Kania*

8

In Uganda, partly as a legacy of war, but also as a result of inadequate access to health care, the number of handicapped people is very large. The World Health Organization (WHO) estimated in 1992 that just under 10 per cent of the Ugandan population (17 million), or about 2 million people, was disabled.[1] On the other hand, the National Union of Disabled Persons of Uganda (NUDIPU) estimates that the total is closer to 15-17 per cent, excluding persons with mental disabilities.[2] However, these may be conservative estimates, given the continuing civil strife in northern Uganda. Moreover, the reduction of discrimination is hampered by the fact that persons with disabilities themselves tend to be seen as the cause of their own problem. Disability is seen to be considered natural and an end in itself, with the result that the disabled community constitutes a segment of the population that is ignored or, at best, sympathized with. Thus, the task of reducing discrimination in employment and integrating persons with disabilities into the workforce is most daunting.

Smaller numbers, but also experiencing discrimination and neglect, are the three principal ethnic minorities in Uganda: the Kebu, the Lendu of the West Nile and the Batwa of Kisoro and Kabale regions. These three minorities, in addition to persons with disabilities, share a sense of marginality in almost all spheres of life in the country. While providing a description of both the constraints and opportunities experienced by each of these categories of persons, this study can only be considered as a broad overview; a detailed analysis of the isolation and other specific impacts of marginality faced by members of each of the categories of persons according to their gender, age, level of education and literacy, as well as the experiences of rural/urban community members, would warrant detailed case-studies in their own right.

I. RATIFICATION OF ILO INSTRUMENTS

Uganda has ratified a number of international labour Conventions and Recommendations which impact directly or indirectly on the situation of persons with disabilities and ethnic minorities, most notably: the Vocational

* Chief Magistrate, Uganda.

Rehabilitation and Employment (Disabled Persons) Convention, 1983 (No. 159); the Employment Policy Convention, 1964 (No. 122) and the Termination of Employment Convention, 1982 (No. 158). Moreover, although the Discrimination (Employment and Occupation) Convention, 1958 (No. 111), has not been ratified, it should be noted that the provisions of Convention No. 158 banning dismissals include the ground of national extraction, thus obliging a ratifying State to ensure that ethnicity is not allowed to influence decisions on termination of a worker's employment.

II. PERSONS WITH DISABILITIES

As noted above, WHO 1992 statistics estimate that Uganda has a significant population of persons with mental handicaps as well as physical disabilities and sensory impairments. Kalinda further categorizes these disabilities into the effects of motor deficiencies, polio, accidents, congenital diseases, mental illness, cerebral palsy, head injuries, brain tumours, and sensory impairments, such as blindness and deafness.[3] Unfortunately, although persons with disabilities have the same needs as non-disabled fellow citizens, disability has been associated in common thinking with curses from the gods and the result of witchcraft, such that parents feel that to attempt to rehabilitate a child would be against the will of the gods. As a result, children with disabilities are always socially isolated; such isolation commences in the home environment, where they are kept segregated from non-disabled children.[4]

An indication of the extent of socio-economic marginalization of persons with disabilities may be had by comparing certain statistical indices. The national literacy rate for the population in general is 56 per cent; the corresponding rate for the disabled community is 3 per cent. The per capita annual income is US$320, whereas it is approximately US$10 for disabled people. Persons with disabilities thus form a disproportionately large segment of the poor, illiterate and unemployed. The number of disabled people who participate in the formal sector is negligible; they are mostly found as self-employed individuals in the urban and rural informal economy. In this regard, a cursory glance at the streets of Kampala and other towns reveals the level of impoverishment of people with disabilities. The majority, especially blind people, live off begging, token fees for drama and musicals, sidewalk vending, shoe-shining and other petty trades in an informal economy having no legislative protection.

The Government has been in the forefront of efforts to institute rehabilitation services and to curb the onset of disabilities. However, major constraints to these initiatives have been the lack of financial resources as well as a lack of infrastructural logistics, especially resulting from the social degeneration which occurred in the 1970s and the imposition of austerity measures affecting rehabilitation schemes during structural adjustment programmes put in place in the 1980s.

The main rehabilitation services furnished by the Government are delivered through the Ministry of Health and the Ministry of Local

Government. They deal mainly with the treatment of polio, orthopaedic workshops, the treatment of ear, nose and throat problems and the training of health professionals such as surgeons, physiotherapists, orthopaedic assistants and occupational therapists. Today, both domestic and international NGOs provide support to the Government in the area of rehabilitation. In this regard, the following organizations could provide a framework for positive measures in favour of their employment: the Uganda Society for Disabled Children (USDC); the Uganda National Association for the Physically Handicapped; the Roman Catholic Church; the Church of Uganda; and the Save the Children Fund. These organizations emphasize medical rehabilitation but also teach vocational skills as well as self-reliance for individuals, groups and guilds.

According to the *National Union of Disabled Persons in Uganda (NUDIPU) News,* the disabled people of Uganda are struggling to organize themselves in order to advance their development.[5] NUDIPU alone has over 40 affiliated associations across the country. These consist of local associations of economically active groups of craft workers, artisans and tradespeople. For example, the Kampala Disabled Peoples' Business Association (KDPBA) was started in 1989 by a group of people with disabilities who operated small enterprises along the capital's streets and verandahs. Notwithstanding the activities of groups such as the KDPBA, greater positive measures of assistance to secure employment, education and proper health-care facilities are needed for disabled persons who seek them.

Another barrier to the integration of disabled persons is the lack of physically accessible buildings and transportation facilities.

The time has come when labour issues can no longer be discussed without taking the situation of persons with disabilities into consideration. The NUDIPU slogan is "Disability is not inability", and in this regard, more aggressive and participatory initiatives are needed from both government and NGOs in order to assist persons with disabilities in securing employment. In this context, support is also needed to improve access to education, and credit for self-employed persons, as well as for those disabled individuals who face additional disadvantage such as women, children and older persons.

Most of the developments in advancing the situation of persons with disabilities have been the result of the peace brought about by the National Resistance Movement Government. However, these efforts have often been misguided, uninformed and haphazard. Coherent legal and socio-economic and political frameworks are needed to address all forms of oppression and discrimination on the grounds of disability. The NUDIPU has enunciated a guiding principle that disabled persons know best their own situation. Faithful to this approach, disabled persons must be active participants in the planning and implementation of national programmes of action.

III. ETHNIC MINORITIES

The Kebu

The Kebu constitute 13 per cent of the population of the region of Uganda known as the West Nile. They trace their origins, according to oral histories, to migrations from Egypt during the period 4000 to 1000 BC, arriving in Uganda from Sudan around the year 1550 AD. They are also said to be part of the following ethnic groups: Negro of Tekru, Mali, Moshi, Hausa, Tezani and Zagawa. Today, they are related to the Landu and Madi of Uganda, as well as the Mural and Avukaya of the Sudan.

Culturally, the Kebu are a patrilineal society in which women are subordinated to men. Traditionally, their economy was based on bartering foodstuffs for other materials. Today, they sell foodstuffs and use the money earned to buy other necessities of life. Among other things, iron tools such as axes and hoes, weapons and jewellery are bartered or exchanged for money. The Kebu's major crops include millet, sorghum, cassava, yams, beans and coffee; a few animals are also kept. It is noted that iron tools and weapons are manufactured by the Kebu using Iron Age technology, and are, therefore, very primitive.

The level of education of the Kebu is very low, and is attributed to the tribalism of their neighbours, the Alur, who discourage their children from attending school. As a result, most of the educated have only primary education, few have reached secondary school, and there are only 20 Kebu who are graduates of university and/or vocational institutes. In addition, the Kebu language remains very marginal.

Only the few educated members of the Kebu ethnic minority are engaged in employment in the formal sector, mainly in teaching. In addition, there is one Kebu medical officer. Other Kebu are engaged in trades such as salesmen and company managers and clerk/administrators. The main employer is the Government.

The Kebu have few services at their disposal. There are 20 primary schools as well as one private secondary school started in 1992 by parents with the assistance of a Netherlands NGO. This ethnic minority has no hospitals or maternity clinics available; the only easily accessible health facility is a grass-thatched dispensary, which lacks drugs.

The Kebu wish the Government and the international community could take the following active, positive measures so as to eliminate their marginalization in the labour market and discrimination against them in employment: create more locally based schools, particularly secondary schools; construct an infrastructure, in particular good roads, bridges and clean water enabling this minority to have access to market-places and enter into exchanges with the rest of the population; supply better public transport; offer grants and subsidies for cash crops; provide more hospitals, clinics and maternity centres, as well as personnel to run them; permit children to be taught in their native language and broadcast native language programmes on the national radio news hour; and increase assistance in job creation, employment and income-generating activities.

To date, the Government has not put in place any structures to ensure equal employment opportunities for the Kebu. Kebu informants indicate that they obtain employment from majority ethnic groups, mostly the Alur, as labourers to clean their coffee plantations. It is reported that only 5 per cent of the Kebu participate in the formal employment sector.

The Batwa

The Batwa pygmy community is principally located in Kisoro Town, a population of approximately 700 out of a total of 80,000 people. The Batwa oral history traces their origins to the Kabale Cyuya forests; they were hunters and also served as soldiers to Rwandese kings.

Economically, the Batwa are engaged in subsistence agriculture, with food-gathering playing a significant part in their activities. Because they do not have land, the Batwa tend to live in temporary structures as squatters at the mercy of landowners. In this regard, the Batwa seek land ownership as a way towards economic and political empowerment. Due to their marginalized conditions, the Batwa do not have access to adequate health facilities and lack clean drinking-water.

Since 1990, programmes were started by a British NGO using churches to encourage the Batwa to send their children to school. However, the effectiveness of this initiative is marginal, as few Batwa attend church. Moreover, those Batwa children who do attend school have experienced harassment and taunting by other students.

A specific example of an affirmative action programme to raise the educational level of the Batwa people may be found in the Kisoro District where a project has resulted in the opening of a primary school for 300 students. The school, which delivers a programme from grades 1 to 4, has six teachers and four ancillary workers.

In view of the extreme marginalization, harassment and neglect faced by the Batwa people, significant assistance is needed from both the Government and the international community, if this ethnic minority is to survive, much less improve its employment potential.

The following recommended measures would help to reduce the level of discrimination in employment experienced by this group, as well as lower their level of social and economic marginalization: land should be demarcated for the Batwa people; settlement camps should be provided, with the aim of eventually apportioning viable parcels of land; adequate free health care should be furnished, including the start of an immunization programme; educational facilities should be constructed and the children encouraged to attend school; and a plan of income-generating activities should be started, and credit provided.

The Lendu

The Lendu are found in Nzugu, Nyoka in Gulu and on the shores of Lake Albert Their oral history indicates that they migrated from ancient Babylon. However, due to a nomadic pattern, an accurate census of their numbers has not been possible; it is thought that there are 3,000 Lendu, occupying five parishes.

Lendu families are headed by men, whose work involves building huts, making granaries, cultivating fields, making iron and wooden instruments and engaging in pit sawing. The women make pots and other household instruments, some of which they sell. On the other hand, many Lendu also work as unskilled labourers for the Alur and Lugbara tribes; others are engaged in metalworking activities.

An issue related to their agricultural activities is the fragmentation of their land. The Lendu lands bordering former Zaire were expropriated by the Government to establish a forest preserve; very little was left for resettlement or agriculture.

Due to their scattered population patterns, some Lendu have become integrated into the tribes of their neighbours, the Alur and Lugbara. The Lendu have no written language, and as a result few of their children attend school. Today, there are only two government-aided primary schools to serve the Lendu population. The Lendu do not have access to health clinics.

The following recommended measures would help to reduce the level of discrimination in employment experienced by the Lendu, as well as improve their level of health and reduce the danger of their assimilation into the Alur and Lugbara tribes: build and equip primary and secondary schools, as well as technical institutes; build a research centre and/or conduct a study to assess the economic viability of establishing an iron-ore industry on Lendu lands; and begin broadcasting in the Lendu language on Radio Uganda.

IV. CONCLUSIONS

This study has described and analysed the problems of the four marginalized groups in Ugandan society: persons with disabilities, and the Kebu, Batwa and Lendu ethnic minorities. While physical impairments and handicaps are the cause of the socio-economic marginalization experienced by disabled people, the problems of the three ethnic minorities are due to their small populations, their general marginalization and their lack of representation at the local and national levels. In all cases, the root of the problem is discrimination in employment and poor or no access to education.

To assist the disabled community and the three ethnic groups in attaining equitable treatment in employment will require a broad-based logistical attack on the infrastructural deficiencies relating to health care and education and sensitizing the broader Ugandan population to the special needs of these four communities. In this regard, it must be recognized that, due to the barriers they experience as a result of their particular situation, it is not enough to treat them the same as the general population of Uganda. Rather, they will need special affirmative action programmes to allow them to arrive at an equitable position when competing for training and employment.

Notes

[1] World Health Organization, 1992.
[2] National Union of Disabled Persons of Uganda (NUDIPU), 1992, p. 6.
[3] Kalinda, 1992.
[4] Mazima, 1992.
[5] NUDIPU, 1993.

CONCLUSIONS

9

In this publication, several differing national affirmative action programmes designed to overcome discrimination experienced by ethnic minorities and persons with disabilities have been presented or proposed. They range from general preferences in education and vocational training places to enterprise-level specific inducements such as tax incentives, wage subsidies and quotas. All imply an effort at sensitizing the general population to the needs and skills of these groups. Indeed, some of the studies list public information campaigns about disabled persons and ethnic minorities as the first leg of state-run affirmative action programmes (Canada, Lebanon, the Russian Federation). Others stress the need for general government measures in the form of land reform, improved physical infrastructure and better active labour market policies as essential "first steps" for any successful affirmative action in the employment field (India, Uganda). Since the number of countries embarking on these schemes is growing, one must ask, in these concluding remarks concerning the national case-studies, whether these programmes actually accomplish what they set out to do and whether any particular model is particularly successful in improving equality in employment for these two groups.

There is no easy answer to this. While the programmes collectively represent an improvement over the situation existing prior to their introduction, the fact is that labour-market experiences of ethnic minorities and persons with disabilities remain inequitable, and this on a worldwide basis.

Instead, what these national case-studies have demonstrated is that the efficacy of affirmative action initiatives must be conceived and put into operation in the light of national circumstances; that there must be adequate support measures in place; and that care must be taken as to whether consensus has been arrived at amongst the national stakeholders.

One initial conclusion is clear: affirmative action models in place in one country cannot be imported to another without taking into consideration the differing national conditions. For example, the Canadian scheme builds on a deeply entrenched system of anti-discrimination legislation which functions in an adversarial system of labour relations. In such a climate, the introduction of imposed "quotas" for persons with disabilities would simply be ineffective. Similarly, the programme in place in Lebanon, based on a combination of both religious and ethnic delineation, is uniquely suited to the circumstances in place in that country. The quota system for civil service posts in place since independence in India has recently received Supreme Court support despite a certain backlash from the non-backward classes; the similar reservation system for Bumiputras established in Malaysia works in favour of an ethnic community which is not a minority but where, in the particular circumstances of that country, the need was felt to redress an historical socio-economic imbalance weighing against that group.

A second conclusion arising from the studies is that, before introducing affirmative action programmes, the existence of support systems must be contemplated. A programme may be very well designed. However, if the public transport system and buildings are not accessible, if outreach programmes are not put in place to address the negative stereotypes and discriminatory attitudes that persons with disabilities and some ethnic minorities face when seeking employment, and if the educational system does not provide the necessary training adapted to the needs of the disabled individual, then the practical result is to limit the effectiveness of the programme's impact.

Support measures also cover what may be styled "national readiness". It is impossible to consider the situations faced by both ethnic minorities and disabled persons outside the context of the socio-political realities of the country. In order to institute positive measures on behalf of marginalized members of society, a prerequisite is a stable social structure which will allow the creation of an economic climate that is propitious to the inclusion of ethnic minorities and disabled persons. This is linked to the comments in several studies that programmes are facing failure or never got off the ground because of insufficient budgets (Lebanon, the Philippines, the Russian Federation).

Thirdly, in order for positive measure programmes to be successful, there must be a national consensus as to the need to institute and maintain such measures. An example of the need to maintain consensus is the situation in Malaysia where it is noted that the Government's affirmative action programme has resulted, after a 20-year period, in "... considerable resentment, especially among the non-Malays, and to a lesser extent, among non-Muslim Bumiputras *(indigens)* as well". The national consensus is often expressed in the adoption of a fundamental law on the subject, such as the Philippine "Magna Carta for the disabled", the 1994 Indian Bill for persons with disabilities and the Lebanese Bill of the same year (both still pending), or the various Philippine Bills under discussion on tribal peoples and the 1994 Russian draft text on the legal status of numerically small native peoples of the north. This text has described these statutory initiatives in some detail, as they highlight common approaches to very diverse situations: these laws will proclaim the fundamental right not to suffer discrimination, along with specific measures for employment and training.

Parallel to this national consensus is a fourth finding: involvement of the stakeholders themselves in the planning, implementation, monitoring and evaluation of affirmative action measures. The Canadian, Indian, Lebanese and Philippine studies bear strong witness to this. Where such measures are working, representatives of the target groups are visible and vocal. Where such representatives are weak, or non-existent, such measures are on shaky ground (Uganda).

Moreover, an adequate understanding of programme parameters on the part of the key stakeholders is critically important. This is a fifth conclusion, drawn from the Canadian, Malaysian and Russian studies. Such a lack of understanding can result at the national level in jealousies and political unreadiness to move ahead with more such measures, and at the enterprise level in a reduced level of management commitment, which manifests itself in a failure to undertake the qualitative equity activities needed to ensure success and a narrow approach to doing the bare minimum in regard to reporting requirements. Similarly, workers' organizations must overcome latent fears of "reverse discrimination" and the notion that affirmative action programmes may in some manner negatively affect seniority and other acquired rights.

The case-studies also give the opportunity to compare approaches to affirmative action in developed and developing countries. Taking Canada as an example of the former, one could summarize its position as follows: legislation has placed equality issues in the forefront of public awareness but for affirmative action in employment to be successful for these two groups, they need to be integrated into all levels of society, and this in turn requires widespread proactive policies in all spheres. Then, taking the Indian study: for success, there is a need for general improvement in social development and for a stronger role for development corporations, NGOs, and representatives of the groups themselves. For countries in transition, the Russian case-study stresses that success is linked to generous social spending. And for countries emerging out of periods of civil strife, the Lebanese study recounts the importance of addressing general issues such as structural development of rehabilitation services, increased training, sensitization of society as a whole, and the adoption and implementation of wide-reaching legislation using input from the target groups themselves.

Lastly, conclusions can be drawn as to the usefulness of international action in this field. It is interesting to note that the various affirmative action measures called for in the conclusions of the case-studies echo, to a large extent, proposals already agreed upon at the international level in relation to one or both of the groups targeted in this publication. For example, the United Nations Standard Rules on the Equalization of Opportunities for Persons with Disabilities, in Rule 1, stresses the importance of awareness-raising in the broadest sense:

1. States should take action to raise awareness in society about persons with disabilities, their rights, their needs, their potential and their contribution.

As with many of the case-studies, it proclaims the need for support services — including assistive devices and equipment for persons with disabilities — so as to enable them to exercise their rights (Rule 4); it highlights access to the physical environment, with organizations of persons with disabilities being consulted when standards in this area are being drawn up (Rule 5); it calls on States to have a clearly stated policy concerning access to education (Rule 6); and, specifically in the area of employment, it makes it clear that laws and regulations should not discriminate against persons with disabilities (backed up by Rule 15 which calls for appropriate sanctions for violations of this principle) and that States should actively support the integration of these persons into the open labour market through measures such as vocational training, incentive-oriented quota schemes, reserved or designated posts, contract compliance, loans or grants for small businesses and tax concessions (Rule 7). Rule 15, on the forms that national legislation for the disabled might take, specifically mentions affirmative action as a possibility. Most importantly, the text calls on States to recognize the organizations of persons with disabilities to represent the disabled at all levels (Rule 18).

Specific United Nations treaty bodies have also made parallel proposals: the Committee on Economic, Social and Cultural Rights in its "General Comment on Persons with Disabilities",[1] after recalling the principle of non-discrimination against the disabled and their integration into the labour market, reminds States of the need to monitor the nature and the scope of the problem, to adopt appropriate policies to respond to these needs, to legislate and eliminate discriminatory laws, to make budgetary provision or seek international assistance to promote the policies and, most importantly for all these measures, to consult with representative groups of those concerned. As regards access to employment, it also stresses the need to remove physical barriers in transport and at the workplace, and to offer vocational training in an integrated setting. Employers should reasonably accommodate the needs of disabled workers.

ILO publications[2] have also suggested measures particularly to eliminate discrimination against the disabled. One publication proposed a Charter for the Disabled in 15 points, including the concept that "mainstreaming" is the best way to promote employment of the disabled, but cautioned that quota laws have only been partially successful.

With countries looking to introduce or develop legislation to eliminate discrimination against the disabled, among others,* this publication has come at an opportune time. The editors trust that the suggestions it contains will help both policy-makers and practitioners, as well as those who use and benefit from the national measures described herein, to advance in the struggle against discrimination in employment.

Notes

[1] United Nations, 1994b.

[2] ILO, 1984, 1985, 1995b, 1996, p. 16; ILO/CEET, 1994.

* The ILO has projects in the pipeline to cover affirmative action for this target group in Angola, Guatemala and Namibia. The United Kingdom also has a new law on the subject.

BIBLIOGRAPHY

Abella, Rosalie Silberman. 1984. *Equality in employment: A Royal Commission Report.* Ottawa, Supply and Services Canada.

ABT Research Associates. 1992a. Final report: *Evaluation of the Federal Contractors Programme.* Submitted to the Programme Evaluation Branch, Employment and Immigration Canada, Ottawa, June.

—. 1992b. *Final report: Evaluation of the Legislated Employment Equity Programme.* Submitted to the Programme Evaluation Branch, Employment and Immigration Canada, Ottawa, June.

Arles, J.-P. 1971. "Ethnic and socio-economic patterns in Malaysia", in *International Labour Review.* Geneva, ILO, Vol. 104, No. 6, Dec.

Arrif, H.Z. 1993. *Role and responsibilities of the Ministry of National Unity and Social Development, Malaysia.* Unpublished paper presented at the Seminar on the Role of the Private Sector in the Socio-economic Uplift of Disabled Persons, Kuala Lumpur, 22-23 Nov.

Ayadurai, D. 1992. *Industrial relations in Malaysia: Law and practice.* Kuala Lumpur, Butterworth Asia.

Bayefsky, Anne; Eberts, Mary. *1985. Equality rights and the Canadian Charter of Rights and Freedoms.* Toronto, Carswell Publishers.

Benimadhu, Prem; Wright, Ruth. *Implementing employment equity, a Canadian experience.* Ottawa. Conference Board of Canada.

Berg, Gracia. 1980. "Lebanon: Composite nation and battleground", in Georgina Ashcroft (ed.) *World minorities in the eighties.* Sunbury, Middlesex, Quartermaine House.

Billingsley, Brenda; Muszynski, Leon. 1985. *No discrimination here? Toronto employers and the multi-racial workforce.* Toronto, Social Planning Council of Metropolitan Toronto.

Bishop, Alan. 1992. *Business consortium on employment equity: Submission to the Office of the Ontario Employment Equity Commissioner.* Toronto, unpublished.

Boyer, Patrick. 1985. *Equality for all; Report of the Parliamentary Committee on Equality Rights.* Ottawa, Queen's Printer for Canada.

Canada. 1984, 1985, 1986. *Employment Equity Act.* Revised Statutes of Canada, 33, 34, 35.

—. 1985. *Canadian Human Rights Act.* Revised Statutes of Canada, c. H-6.

Canadian Advisory Council on the Status of Women. 1992. "A brief to the Special House of Commons Committee on the Review of the Employment Equity Act". Unpublished brief, Ottawa, 18 Mar.

Canadian Human Rights Commission. 1990. *Unequal access: An accessibility survey of selected federal government offices, report #1.* Ottawa.

—. 1991a. *Annual Report, 1990.* Ottawa, Supply and Services, 1991(a).

—. 1991b. *Unequal access: Availability of federal government publications in alternate format, report #2.* Ottawa.

—. 1991c. Unequal access: *Availability of TDD services by federal departments, report #3.* Ottawa.

—. 1992a. *The Canadian Human Rights Commission and employment equity, 1987-1991, A background paper.* Ottawa.

—. 1992b. *Unequal access: An accessibility survey of selected banks, report #41.* Ottawa.

—. 1992c. *Unequal access: An accessibility survey of selected postal outlets, report #5.* Ottawa.

—. 1994. *Annual Report, 1993.* Ottawa, Supply and Services Canada.

—; Saskatchewan Wheat Pool. 1992. Joint agreement, 21 Apr.

Canadian National Railways Company. 1993. "1993 Annual employer's report for the year ending December 31, 1992". Unpublished report submitted by Canadian National Railways pursuant to the Employment Equity Act.

Canadian Recruiters Guild. 1987. *A survey on employment discrimination in Canada.* Ottawa.

Caritas (International Confederation of Catholic Organizations for Charitable and Social Action), Lebanon branch. 1993. *Les handicapés au Liban.* Study conducted by Issam Ikiki. Beirut.

Centre for Community Studies. 1994. *Orang Aslis and Development.* Kuala Lumpur.

Chew, P.H. 1992. *The mentally handicapped: Their vocational competency and employers' attitudes.* Unpublished Masters thesis, Department of Anthropology and Sociology, University of Malaya.

Ching, C. 1991. *Dynamics of the current labour market and its implications for workers.* Unpublished paper presented at the National Tripartite Seminar on Labour Market Information, Petaling Jaya, Malaysia, 20-21 Nov.

Chua, J.M. 1991. *The goods and strategies of the national development policy.* Unpublished paper presented at the Malaysian Chinese Assembly, Kuala Lumpur, 25 Aug.

Chua, Y.Y. 1991. *The economic policies after the New Economic Policy.* Unpublished paper presented at the Malaysian Chinese Assembly, Kuala Lumpur, 16 June.

Decima Research Company, 1992a. *Focus group report for the Department of the Secretary of State.* Ottawa, Decima Research Company.

—. 1992b. *Interviews with business and media representatives: A Decima Research report to the Secretary of State.* Ottawa, Decima Research Company.

Doyle, B. 1993. "Employment rights, equal opportunities and disabled persons: The ingredients of reform", in *Industrial Law Journal.* London, Vol. 22, No. 2, June.

—. 1996. "Disabled workers' rights, the Disability Discrimination Act and UN standard rules", in *Industrial Law Journal.* London, Vol. 25, No. 1, Mar.

Dubar, Claude; Nasr, Salin. 1976. *Les classes sociales au Liban.* Paris, Presse de la Fondation nationale des sciences politiques.

Employment and Immigration Advisory Council. 1991. *Immigrants and language training.* Ottawa, Employment and Immigration Canada.

Employment and Immigration Canada. 1986. *Employment Equity Act, Regulations and schedules.* Ottawa, Supply and Services Canada.

—. 1987 *Federal Contractors Programme: Information for suppliers.* Ottawa, Supply and Services Canada.

—. 1991a. "Landings by world area, January to December, 1989 and 1990". Ottawa.

—. 1991b. "Landings from 20 major source countries, January to December, 1989 and 1990". Ottawa.

—. 1991c. *New immigrant language training policy.* Policy position report of the Immigration Policy and Programme Development Branch. Ottawa.

—. 1991d. "Consultations in preparation for the review of the Employment Equity Act". Ottawa, Supply and Services Canada.

—. 1992 "Language training policy". Minister's Press Release (92-2). Statement of the Honourable Bernard Valcour, Minister of Employment and Immigration. Ottawa.

Faundez, J. *Affirmative action: International perspectives.* Geneva, ILO.

Ganapathy, R. *The placement of disabled persons in employment: Some problems and strategies.* Unpublished paper presented at the Seminar on Education and Training of the Handicapped and their Integration into the Labour Market, Kuala Lumpur, 27-28 Oct.

Goh, C.T. 1994. *Malaysia beyond communal politics.* Petaling Jaya, Malaysia, Pelanduk Publications.

Government of India. 1992a. *The National Sample Survey on Disability.* New Delhi.

—. 1992b. *Gazette of India.* The Rehabilitation Council of India Act, No. 34 of 1992, New Delhi, 2 Sep.

—. 1996. The Persons with Disabilities (Equal Opportunities, Protection of Rights and Full Participation) Act, No. 1 of 1996. New Delhi, 1 Jan.

Government of India Department of Social Welfare. 1977. *Concessions and programmes for the physically handicapped.* New Delhi, Sep.

—. 1986. *Uniform definitions of the physically handicapped.* Combined reports of three committees set up for the purpose of identification of disabilities and job relevance. New Delhi, Aug.

—. 1987. *Scheme of assistance to organizations for the disabled persons.* New Delhi.

Henry, F. 1989. "Who gets the work in 1989?". Unpublished report prepared for the Economic Council of Canada, Toronto.

—; Ginzberg, E. *Who gets the work? A test of racial discrimination in employment.* Toronto, Social Planning Council of Metropolitan Toronto.

Holmes, L. 1994. Special Policy Advisor, Settlement Branch, Canadian Department of Citizenship and Immigration, interviewed by C. Raskin, Ottawa.

Howell, S. 1994. Equal Opportunities Officer, Canadian Union of Public Employees (CUPA), interviewed by C. Raskin, Ottawa.

Human Resources Development Canada. 1993. *Annual Report, Employment Equity Act, 1993.* Ottawa, Minister of Supply and Services.

Husseini, H.; Houri, M. 1982. *A summary report on preliminary study of disabled people in Lebanon.* Beirut.

ILO. 1984. *International labour standards on vocational rehabilitations: Guidelines for implementation.* Geneva.

—. 1985. *Basic principles of vocational rehabilitation of the disabled (3rd (revised) ed.).* Geneva.

—. 1988. *Equality in employment and occupation, General Survey by the Committee of Experts on the Application of Conventions and Recommendations.* International Labour Conference, 75th Session, Report III (Part 4B), Geneva.

—. 1993. *Equitable training and employment opportunities for disabled persons.* Unpublished position paper of the Vocational Rehabilitation Branch, Geneva.

—. 1994. *Report of the Committee of Experts on the Application of Conventions and Recommendations.* International Labour Conference, 81st Session, Report III (Part 4A), Geneva.

—. 1995a. *Report of the Committee of Experts on the Application of Conventions and Recommendations.* International Labour Conference, 82nd Session, Report III (Part 4A), Geneva.

—. 1995b. *Gender issues in the world of work: Gender training package.* Geneva.

—. 1996. *Employment prospects for disabled people in transition countries.* Geneva.

ILO/Central Eastern European Multidisciplinary Team (CEET). 1994. *Disabled workers in Central and Eastern Europe: A policy manual.* Budapest, Jan.

International Work Group for Indigenous Affairs. 1995. *The indigenous world.* Copenhagen.

Jain, H.; Hackett, R.D. 1991. *A comparison of employment equity and non-employment equity organizations on designated group representation and views towards staffing.* McMaster University Faculty of Business Working Paper 367, Hamilton, Ontario.

Jayasooria, D. et al. 1992. "Disabled persons, the caring society and policy recommendations for the 1990s and beyond", in K.S. Cho and I.M. Salleh (eds.): *Caring society, emerging issues and future directions.* Kuala Lumpur, ISIS.

Jomo, K.S. 1989. *Beyond 1990: Considerations for a new national development strategy.* Kuala Lumpur, University of Malaysia.

—. 1993. *Industrializing Malaysia: Policy, performance, prospects.* London, Routledge.

—. 1994. *Malaysia's economy in the nineties.* Petaling Jaya, Malaysia, Pelanduk Publications.

Kalinda, N. 1992. Collection of background information on rehabilitation programmes in Uganda, community-based rehabilitation and national programmes. Mulago Hospital, Kampala, 17 June.

Kelley, K. 1994. Analyst, Employment Equity Data Programme, Statistics Canada, interviewed by C. Raskin, 1994.

Kelly, J. 1991. *Human resource management and the human rights process.* Don Mills, Ontario, CCH Canadian Ltd.

Kinan, N. 1993. Paper presented at the National Conference on Disability, 23 Apr.

Koyakoti, M.S. 1981. *Ethnic representation in the economy of a plural society: A case-study of employment under the Malaysian New Economic Policy.* Unpublished doctoral dissertation, Albany, State University of New York.

Labine, J. 1994. Women's Programme Officer, Public Service Alliance of Canada, interviewed by C. Raskin, Ottawa.

Landorganisasjonen (National Labour Organization), 1992a. *Typisk norsk å være god? Om bruk av utlendingers kompetanse i arbeidslivet [Is it unusual for Norwegians to be good? Using the skills and knowledge of foreigners in employment].* Oslo.

—. 1992b. *Handlingsplan 1993-97 [Plan of Action 1993-97],* Oslo.

Leck, J.D.; Saunders, D.M. 1991. *Compliance with the Canadian Employment Equity Act: A model and empirical test.* Paper presented at the Annual Conference of the Law and Society Association. Amsterdam.

Lunt, N.; Thornton, P. 1993. *Employment policies for disabled people: A review of legislation and services in fifteen countries.* Research Series 16, London, Department of Employment.

Mahathir, M. 1991. Speech at Parliament. *New Straits Times.* June 18.

Malaysia. 1991. *The Second Outline Perspective Plan 1991-2000.* Kuala Lumpur, Government Printers.

—. 1992. *National Labour Policy*. Kuala Lumpur, Ministry of Human Resources.

Malaysia Department of Statistics. 1995. *Yearbook of Statistics, 1994*. Kuala Lumpur, Oct.

Malaysian Indian Congress, 1992. *The second round, Vision 2000 and Malaysian Indians*. Kuala Lumpur.

Mazima, E. 1992. *The handicapped child*. Presentation at ANPPAN seminar on child abuse and neglect, Uganda chapter, 22 Jan.

McDade, K. 1988. *Barriers to recognition of the credentials of immigrants in Canada*. Ottawa, Institute for Research on Public Policy.

McDowell, D. 1996. "Lebanon: A conflict of minorities", Report of the Minority Rights Group (MRG), in *Manchester Free Press*. Manchester, Feb.

McInnes, R. 1992. Proceedings of testimony before the House of Commons Special Committee on the Review of the Employment Equity Act. Ottawa, 9 Mar.

—. 1994. Executive Director, Canadian Centre for Rehabilitation and Work, interviewed by C. Raskin, Winnipeg.

Mills, C.P. 1984. "Industrial disputes law in Malaysia", in *Malaysian Law Journal*. (Kuala Lumpur.

Minority Rights Group (MRG). 1988. *The Saami of Lapland* (2nd ed.). London.

Molloy, A. 1992. "Disability and the duty to accommodate", in *Canadian Law Journal*. Markham, Ontario, Butterworth, Vol. 1-2, spring/summer.

Mosaikk [Mosaic]. 1993. Oslo, Utlendingsdirektoratet [Foreigners Directorate], No. 2.

—. 1994. Oslo, OECD. Utlendingsdirektoratet [Foreigners Directorate], No. 2.

Muzaffar, C. 1987. "The protection of minorities: The Malaysian position", in *INSAF: The Journal of the Malaysian Bar*. Kuala Lumpur, Vol. XX, No. 2.

National Union of Disabled Persons of Uganda (NUDIPU), 1992. *National Union of Disabled Persons of Uganda (NUDIPU) News*. Kampala, Feb.

—. 1993. *National Union of Disabled Persons of Uganda (NUDIPU) News*. Kampala, Sep.

Official Bulletin. 1959. Vol. XLII, No. 7. Geneva, ILO.

Onyalo, D. 1994. National Representative, Canadian Labour Congress, interviewed by C. Raskin, Ottawa.

Organisation for Economic Co-operation and Development (OECD). 1992. *Employment policies for people with disabilities, Report by an evaluation panel*. Paris.

Ontario. 1981. *Ontario Human Rights Code*. Statutes of Ontario, Ch. 53, amended 1990, Ch. 15, section 65.

Ontario Advisory Council for Disabled Persons. 1990. *Workable: Fulfilling the potential of people with disabilities*. Toronto.

Phillips, R. 1992-94. Chief, Employment Equity, Canadian Human Rights Commission, interviewed by C. Raskin, Ottawa.

Rådet for Funksjonshemmede. 1990. *Funksjonshemming: levekår og rettigheter [Disability: Living conditions and rights]*. Oslo.

—. 1993. *Presentasjon av rådet, arbeidsprogram 1992-95, tiltak 1994, årsmedling 1993 [Presentation of the Council, Work Programme for 1992-95 and Annual Report 1993]*. Oslo.

Ramachandran, S. 1994. *Indian plantation labour in Malaysia*. Kuala Lumpur, INSAN.

Ramasamy, P. 1994. *The state, unions and plantation labour in Malaysia*. Oxford, Oxford University Press.

Raskin, C. 1993. *De facto discrimination, immigrant workers and ethnic minorities: A Canadian overview*. Geneva, ILO.

Rebick, J.; Poole, P. 1992 "Not another hundred years: NAC brief to the Parliamentary Committee Reviewing the Employment Equity Act." Unpublished brief of the National Action Committee on the Status of Women, Toronto, Jan.

Redway, A. 1992. *A matter of fairness.* Report of the Special Committee on the Review of the Employment Equity Act, Ottawa, Supply and Services Canada.

Robb, A.L.; Robb, R.M. 1993. "Employment equity and competitiveness, final report". Unpublished study prepared for Employment and Immigration Canada, Ottawa, June.

Roeher Institute. 1992. *On target? Canada's employment-related programmes for persons with disabilities.* Toronto.

Royal Bank of Canada. 1993. "1993 Annual employer's report for the year ending December 31, 1992". Unpublished report submitted by Canadian National Railways pursuant to the Employment Equity Act.

Samual, T. John. 1989-90. "Immigration, visible minorities and labour force in Canada: Vision 2000", in *Journal of Intergroup Relations.* Ottawa, Vol. XVI, Nos. 3-4, fall/winter.

Shari, S. 1980. *Economic development and employment policies in Malaysia.* Unpublished paper presented at ICFTU/ARO Expert Meeting on Employment Policies, Bangkok, 26-30 Aug.

Statens Trykksaksekspedisjon [Trykksakseksp State Editors]. 1993. *Regjeringens handlingsplan for funksjonshemmede 1994-97 [Government National Plan of Action for Disabled Persons 1994-97],* Oslo.

Statistics Canada. 1991. *Health and activity limitation survey — 1991 user's guide.* Ottawa.

—. 1993. "The Daily", Ontario, 27 July.

Suffian. 1976. *An introduction to the Constitution of Malaysia.* Kuala Lumpur, Government Printers.

Tarnopolsky, Walter S. 1979. *Discrimination and affirmative action: American experience and application in Canada.* Unpublished.

Tør vi satse på en innvander [Can we count on immigrants?]. 1992. Gjøvik, Kallerud kurs or konferansesenter a/s [Kallerud Course and Conference Materials Pty. Ltd.].

Tellier, M. 1994. Vice-President, Employment Equity, Canadian National Railways, interviewed by C. Raskin, Montreal.

Treasury Board of Canada. 1993. *Distortions in the mirror: Reflections of visible minorities in the public service of Canada.* Ottawa.

—. 1994. *Case-studies on effective practices in the employment of persons with disabilities,* .Ottawa.

Uganda Ministry of Finance and Economic Planning. 1992. Final results of 1991 population and housing census. Kampala.

Uganda Ministry of Labour and Social Welfare. 1992. Proposals to the Constitutional Commission by the Labour Department, Kampala.

United Nations. 1982. Doc. A/37/351/Add.1 and Corr.1, Adopted by the General Assembly in resolution 37/52. 3 Dec.

—. 1993a. Doc. E/1990/5/Add.1/6. 6 July.

—. 1993b. General Assembly resolution 48/96. 20 Dec.

—. 1994a. Doc. E/1994/104/add. 3. 15 Sep.

—. 1994b. Doc. E/C.12/1994/13. 14 Dec.

White, L. 1994. Manager, Employment Equity, Royal Bank of Canada, interviewed by C. Raskin, Montreal.

White, R. 1994. President, Canadian Labour Congress. Keynote address, 1994 Canadian Labour Congress Human Rights Conference. Ottawa, 27 and 28 Feb. and 1 Mar.

World Health Organization (WHO). 1980. *International Classification of Impairments, Disabilities and Handicaps: A manual of classification relating to the consequences of disease.* Geneva.

—. 1992. *Prevalence of disability in Uganda.* Geneva.

Zegers de Beijl, R. 1991. "Discrimination of migrant workers in Western Europe". World Employment Programme Working Paper No. 49. Geneva, ILO.